NEVER ALONE

VOLUME 1

Walking with Jesus:
Living the Life God Created You For

Pamela D White

Copyright © 2026 by Pamela D White

All Rights Reserved.

No part of this book may be reproduced or transmitted in any form or by any means, electronic or mechanical—including photocopying, recording, or by any information storage and retrieval system—without permission in writing from the publisher. Please direct inquiries to Blooming Desert Ministries.

ISBN 978-1-7362017-7-0

Published and distributed by IngramSparks (Lightning Source, LLC)

One Ingram Blvd., La Vergne, TN 37086

A publication of Blooming Desert Ministries, an imprint of PDW Publications.

Printed in the United States of America

All scripture quotations, unless otherwise indicated, are taken from the Holy Bible, **New King James Version©**. Copyright © 1982 by Thomas Nelson, Inc. Used by permission. All rights reserved.

Scripture quotations marked NIV are taken from the Holy Bible, **New International Version** ®, NIV ®. Copyright © 1973, 1978, 1984 by **Biblica, Inc.® Used by permission. All rights reserved worldwide.**

Scripture quotations marked NASB are taken from the Holy Bible, **New American Standard Bible®,** Copyright © 1960, 1971, 1977, 1995, 2020 by The Lockman Foundation. All rights reserved.

Scripture quotations marked AMP are taken from the Holy Bible, **Amplified**, copyright © 2015 by The Lockman Foundation, La Habra, CA 90631. All rights reserved. For Permission To Quote information visit http://www.lockman.org/

Scripture quotations marked ESV are taken from the ESV® Bible (The Holy Bible, **English Standard Version®**). ESV® Text Edition: 2016. Copyright © 2001 by Crossway, a publishing ministry of Good News Publishers. The ESV® text has been reproduced in cooperation with and by permission of Good News Publishers. Unauthorized reproduction of this publication is prohibited. All rights reserved.

Scripture quotations marked NLT are taken from the Holy Bible, **New Living Translation,** copyright © 1996, 2004, 2015 by Tyndale House Foundation. Used by permission of Tyndale House Publishers, Inc., Carol Stream, Illinois 60188. All rights reserved.

Scripture quotations marked MSG are taken from **THE MESSAGE**, copyright © 1993, 2002, 2018 by Eugene H. Peterson. Used by permission of NavPress. All rights reserved. Represented by Tyndale House Publishers, Inc.

Scripture quotations marked AKJV are taken from the Holy Bible, **Authorized King James Version**, The Authorized (King James) Version of the Bible ('the KJV'), the rights in which are vested in the Crown in the United Kingdom, is reproduced here by permission of the Crown's patentee, Cambridge University Press. The Cambridge KJV text, including paragraphing, is reproduced here by permission of Cambridge University Press.

Scripture quotations marked KJV are taken from the Holy Bible, **King James Version**.

Cover design and interior formatting by independent design professionals.

Publishing Note: This book follows a style that capitalizes pronouns referring to the Father, Son, and Holy Spirit in Scripture quotations, which may differ from other publishing conventions. Emphasis within Scripture quotations is the author's. The name satan and related names are intentionally not capitalized as a stylistic choice reflecting the author's perspective.

Table of Contents

- ✦ Preface — vii
- ✦ Quick Guide: How to Use This Book — ix

Part I: There Must Be a Better Way — 1
Walking in Salvation

1. What is Salvation? — 5
2. Walking in Righteousness — 17
3. Transformation — 22
4. Understanding Salvation — 27
5. The Finished Work of Christ — 36
6. You Are an Eternal Being — 43
7. Confession of Faith — 48
8. Tools to Help You Walk Out Your Salvation — 52
9. Stepping Stones — 57

Part II: Lord, I Need Help! — 61
Walking With the Holy Spirit

10. Who Is the Holy Spirit? — 64
11. Getting to Know the Holy Spirit — 71
12. What Does the Holy Spirit Do? — 77
13. Filled With the Holy Spirit — 83
14. Yielding to the Holy Spirit — 87
15. Tools to Live Holy With the Holy Spirit — 93
16. Stepping Stones — 98

Part III: I Thought I Was Changed — 101
Walking in Transformation

17. The Power to Break Free — 104
18. You Are a Three-Part Being — 108

19.	Your Second Chance	112
20.	Making Choices to Grow and Mature	116
21.	How to Free the Body and Soul	121
22.	Results of Transformation	128
23.	The Benefits of Growing in Christ	134
24.	Stepping Stones	139

Part IV: I Am Empowered — 143
Walking in Spiritual Gifts

25.	Purpose of Spiritual Gifts	146
26.	Activating Spiritual Gifts	152
27.	Manifestation or Expression of Spiritual Gifts	156
28.	Power Gifts of the Spirit	164
29.	Gifts of Inspiration	172
30.	Motivational Gifts	179
31.	Ministry Gifts	188
32.	Discovering Spiritual Gifts	196
33.	Using Your Gifts with Confidence	200
34.	Stepping Stones	207

✦ Preface

If you are holding this book, I believe you're not here by accident.

This book was born out of my own journey with God—through questions, struggles, and a deep desire to know Him more. I didn't begin by planning a study or workbook; I began by searching the Scriptures for myself. I needed answers when life felt overwhelming, when I doubted my own strength, and when I wondered if God's promises were really for me. What I discovered, page by page, was that His Word is alive, and His Spirit still speaks today.

What you'll find in these chapters is not a list of rules or a heavy burden to carry. It's a journey—rooted in salvation, shaped by the presence of the Holy Spirit, and grounded in the truth of who God created you to be. This volume is meant to help you begin living the life God designed for you, one step at a time.

But more than information, this is an invitation: to walk with Jesus. To know Him not as an idea or tradition, but as a living Savior, Friend, and King. Along the way, you'll find reflection questions, practical tools, and stepping stones—because my prayer is that this book won't just be read, but lived.

Take it slowly. Don't rush through the pages. Let the Word breathe over you. Sometimes one verse, one phrase, or one whisper from the Holy

Spirit is enough to carry you for days. That's the point—this isn't about finishing quickly, but about meeting God in His Word and letting Him transform your heart.

I don't know what you're carrying as you begin this journey, but I do know this: the same God who met me will meet you. And He delights to walk with you, one step at a time.

This journey is not about having all the answers—it is about discovering you are never walking alone.

Welcome to the journey.

Pam

✦ Quick Guide: How to Use This Book

Here are a few ways to make the most of what's inside these pages. This volume is designed to help you begin living the life God created for you; you don't need to do everything at once.

- **Pray First**—Ask the Holy Spirit to guide you as you read.
- **Read Slowly**—Don't rush; let the Word sink in.
- **Practice Memory Verses**—Say them out loud and write them down.
- **Reflect & Journal**—Use the questions to apply truth to your own life.
- **Pray with Guidance**—Follow the guided prayers at the end of each part.
- **Dig Deeper**—Look up the extra Scriptures for stronger roots.
- **Carry the Truths**—Review the "10 Truths to Carry With You" summaries.
- **Go at Your Own Pace**—This is not a race; it's a journey.
- **Study Alone or in a Group**—Both work—choose what fits your season.

✨ Remember: the goal isn't finishing quickly, but growing closer to Jesus step by step.

PART I

There Must Be a Better Way

Walking in Salvation

"For whoever calls on the name of the Lord shall be saved."

—Romans 10:13 (NKJV)

🎯 Objective

This lesson lays a biblical foundation for understanding salvation. It will help you grasp God's plan—not just to save you from sin, but to bring you back into relationship with Himself.

From the beginning, God's desire has been to walk with His people. But sin separated us from that closeness. Every one of us is born with a natural pull toward selfishness—that's the sin-nature. You've probably seen those shows about extreme makeovers or extreme couponing. Sin-nature is like extreme selfishness—it takes over without you even trying.

But salvation changes everything.

Through Jesus Christ, you are invited into a new way of living—free from the grip of sin, and growing in love, humility, and purpose. This lesson will equip you with spiritual tools to walk out your salvation day by day, growing in your relationship with God and becoming more like Christ.

———————◆———————

📖 Memory Verses

> "For whoever calls on the name of the Lord shall be saved."
> —Romans 10:13 (NKJV)

> "For all have sinned and fall short of the glory of God."
> —Romans 3:23 (NKJV)

✿ Introduction

We all come to a moment when we know something has to change.

Maybe life feels heavy, or confusing. Maybe you're tired of running in circles, trying to fix what keeps falling apart. Maybe you've looked around and thought:

"There has to be a better way to live than this."

That longing is not weakness—it's your spirit responding to the call of your Creator.

The better way isn't a secret, and it isn't found in striving harder. The better way is a person.

His name is Jesus.

In the Bible, the word "salvation" means deliverance—being rescued from the power of sin and brought into eternal life. It's not just about what happens after you die. It's about living free and whole *now*—walking with the One who created you, knows you, and loves you without conditions.

When you walk with Jesus, your life doesn't suddenly become perfect. But it becomes **possible**—possible to live with purpose, peace, and power even in the middle of hard things. This journey isn't about becoming someone else. It's about becoming the person God designed you to be from the beginning.

So if you're searching for answers, longing for more, or just trying to make sense of what salvation really means, you're in the right place.

You were made for relationship with God. You were made to walk with Jesus. And there is a better way.

Let's find it together.

1.
What is Salvation?

✦ What is Salvation?

Salvation is more than just going to heaven someday. It's the beginning of a relationship—a personal rescue, a spiritual rebirth, and an invitation to walk in freedom with God starting now. Salvation means being rescued and restored to relationship with God through faith in Jesus Christ. The Bible also calls this being "born again" or "made new."

From the very beginning, God's plan for you never included sin, separation, or death. He created the earth and placed humankind in a perfect place—a garden filled with life, beauty, and communion with Him. But then came the lie. The enemy deceived Adam and Eve, and in a moment of disobedience, humanity was pulled out of harmony with God. (see Genesis 1–3)

That choice—the fall—brought sin and death into the world. Every child born after that moment (including you and me) inherited that brokenness. We were made in God's image, but we were born disconnected from Him. The story of salvation is how God, in His love, made a way to restore what was lost.

✦ God's Rescue Plan

You don't have to drown.

That might sound dramatic, but it's the truth. The world is flooded with pain, fear, shame, and confusion—and many people are just trying to stay afloat. They keep treading water, hoping something better will come along. But what if the rescue already arrived?

There's an old story you may have heard. A man was caught in a terrible flood. As the water rose, a neighbor in a rowboat came by and offered to take him to safety. "No thanks," the man said. "God will save me."

Later, a rescue team in a motorboat came by and pleaded with him to come aboard. "I'm trusting God," he insisted. "He'll save me."

Finally, a helicopter hovered above and dropped a ladder, urging him to climb up. But again, he refused. "God's got me. I have faith."

Eventually, the man drowned.

When he stood before God, he asked, "Why didn't You save me?"

God replied, "I sent you a rowboat, a motorboat, and a helicopter. What more were you waiting for?"

It's a funny story—until you realize how many of us are doing the same thing. We cry out for help, but then overlook the rescue plan because it doesn't look the way we expected. We think God's help should feel more magical, more dramatic. We wait for thunder from heaven… while quietly ignoring the boat that's already floating in our direction.

God's rescue plan isn't always loud—but it is real.

God didn't abandon us. He saw the flood of sin and brokenness in the world, and He didn't leave us to figure it out on our own. He sent His Son,

Jesus, to rescue us. Not with flashing lights or sirens—but with love. He stepped into our mess, took our sin, and made a way for us to be made new. He died in our place so that we could live in His.

Salvation isn't something you earn. It's something you receive. It's a gift bought by the blood of Jesus—a gift that brings you back into relationship with your Creator and offers you the full inheritance of being part of God's family. The cross wasn't just a symbol. It was a lifeline.

> "But God showed His great love for us by sending Christ to die for us while we were still sinners."
>
> —Romans 5:8 (NLT)

✦ The Big Picture of Salvation

Let's break it down:

- **Salvation is God's plan** to rescue you from sin and spiritual death.
- **Spiritual death** means being eternally separated from God. That's far more devastating than physical death.
- **Repentance** is part of salvation. It means turning away from sin completely—a change of heart and direction.
- **Freedom from sin** is what salvation brings. Just like God delivered the Israelites from slavery in Egypt, Jesus delivers us from the slavery of sin.
- **Jesus Christ is the source** of salvation. His perfect sacrifice paid the price for our rescue and reconnected us with God.

> "For God so loved the world, that He gave His only begotten Son, that whoever believes in Him should not perish but have everlasting life."
>
> —John 3:16 (KJV)

✦ How Do I Know I'm Saved?

A preacher once said, *"You can sit in a garage and call yourself a car, but that doesn't make you one."* The same is true with salvation. You can call yourself a Christian, go to church, do good deeds, and still not experience the saving relationship God offers through Jesus Christ.

Salvation isn't just a label—it's a transformation.

So how do you know if it's real? How do you know you've truly been saved?

✦ Biblical Markers of Salvation

Here are some key signs that confirm salvation has taken root in your life:

- **You've confessed Jesus as your Lord and Savior.**

    "If you confess with your mouth the Lord Jesus and believe in your heart that God has raised Him from the dead, you will be saved."

    —Romans 10:9–10 (NKJV)

- **You believe in the life, death, and resurrection of Jesus.** This belief isn't just intellectual—it's something you trust and build your life around.
- **Your spirit is being renewed.** There's a shift inside you. You're not perfect, but your desires begin to change. What once felt normal may now feel out of place. That's the Spirit of God working in you.

✦ A Historic Declaration of Faith

In many churches, believers recite something called the *Apostles' Creed*—an early and powerful statement of faith. It captures the core of what Christians believe:

**I believe in God the Father Almighty, Maker of heaven and earth.
And in Jesus Christ, His only Son, our Lord;
Who was conceived by the Holy Spirit, born of the Virgin Mary,
suffered under Pontius Pilate, was crucified, died, and was buried;
He descended into hell; the third day He rose again from the dead;
He ascended into heaven and sits at the right hand of God the
Father Almighty;
From there He will come to judge the living and the dead.
I believe in the Holy Spirit, the holy Christian Church, the
communion of saints,
the forgiveness of sins, the resurrection of the body, and the life
everlasting. Amen.**

It's one thing to say these words. It's another to *believe* them. **Salvation makes it possible not only to speak these truths—but to live like they're real.**

✦ Resting in the Assurance of Salvation

Salvation isn't something fragile that slips away when you struggle or doubt. It's a covenant sealed by God Himself. You didn't earn it, and you don't have to fear losing it. Once you have placed your faith in Jesus, your salvation is secure—not because you'll never stumble, but because He will never let you go.

> *"He who began a good work in you will carry it on to completion until the day of Christ Jesus."*
>
> —Philippians 1:6 (NIV)

When you fall, grace is there to lift you. When you feel uncertain, the Holy Spirit reminds your heart that you belong to God. Assurance doesn't come from being perfect—it comes from trusting the One who is.

✦ What Changes When I Receive Christ's Salvation?

When you accept salvation, something shifts. The change may not always be dramatic on the outside—but on the inside, a brand-new life has begun.

Salvation isn't just a moment—it's the start of a transformation. Here are two powerful, biblical truths that take place the moment you believe:

1. You Become a New Creation

When you place your faith in Jesus, you are made spiritually new. You may look the same on the outside. Your thoughts and habits might still feel familiar. But your **spirit**—the part of you that connects with God—is completely reborn.

> "Therefore, if anyone is in Christ, he is a new creation; old things have passed away; behold, all things have become new."
>
> —2 Corinthians 5:17 (NKJV)

The "old you" no longer defines you. That doesn't mean you won't struggle—but it means sin no longer has the final say. You've been given a new nature. A new heart. A new start.

2. God's Spirit Lives in You

When you're saved, the Holy Spirit takes up residence in your life. He doesn't just visit—you become His dwelling place. His presence begins to shape your thinking, comfort you in pain, and guide your steps.

And even when you doubt or feel unworthy, the Spirit reminds your heart: **You belong to God now.**

"The Spirit Himself bears witness with our spirit that we are children of God."

—Romans 8:16 (NKJV)

You now have a perfect Father who will never leave you. He doesn't disown you when you mess up. He draws you near. He calls you His—even when you forget who you are.

✦ Why Do I Need Salvation?

It's a fair question. If God is loving and good, why can't we just live a decent life, try our best, and hope that's enough?

The answer is rooted in truth—and in love.

✦ The Problem: Separation from God

God created us for relationship with Him. From the very beginning, His plan was closeness, not distance. He formed Adam and Eve, the first man and woman, and placed them in a beautiful garden where they could live in peace, purpose, and unbroken connection with their Creator.

But He also gave them something sacred: the ability to choose.

God placed a tree in the middle of the garden—the Tree of the Knowledge of Good and Evil—and told them not to eat from it. This wasn't just about fruit. It was about trust. Would they trust that God's way was best, or would they choose to go their own way?

Tempted by the serpent (Satan), Adam and Eve chose to disobey. They took the fruit, ate it, and tried to hide from God. In that moment, sin entered the world—not just as an action, but as a condition. That first act of disobedience broke something deep. It broke their closeness with God, introduced shame and fear, and allowed death—both physical and spiritual—to enter the human story.

They didn't just break a rule.

They broke relationship.

And that brokenness has been passed down to every generation since. Every lie, every selfish choice, every moment we push God aside and do things our own way—all of it flows from that same fracture.

Sin separates.

It's like a wall between you and the One who made you. You can't climb over it with good deeds or fix it with positive thoughts. You can't outrun it, outgrow it, or ignore it long enough to make it disappear. Only God can tear the wall down.

> "But your iniquities have separated you from your God, and your sins have hidden His face from you, so that He will not hear."
>
> —Isaiah 59:2 (NKJV)

✦ The Law of Sin is Like Gravity

You can't "try harder" to escape sin, just like you can't jump your way out of gravity.

You might temporarily feel like you're rising above it—through success, distraction, or even religion—but eventually, the weight pulls you back down.

But there is good news: **Jesus broke the power of sin.**

Like a rocket breaking through Earth's atmosphere, Jesus made a way for you to be free—permanently.

Through Him, you're no longer stuck in the downward pull of sin and spiritual death.

> "For the wages of sin is death, but the gift of God is eternal life in Christ Jesus our Lord."
>
> —Romans 6:23 (NKJV)

✦ Two Deaths—or One Life

Every person will face a physical death. These earthly bodies were never meant to last forever. But Scripture teaches that without salvation, we also face something far more serious: a second death.

1. **The first death** is physical—it happens when your body dies and your time on earth ends.
2. **The second death** is spiritual—eternal separation from God, where the soul is cut off from His presence, love, and life. It is the final consequence of rejecting His rescue plan.

This isn't God's desire for anyone. Hell was never created for people—it was prepared for the devil and his angels (see Matthew 25:41). But when someone refuses the gift of salvation, they choose to remain separated from God, even after death.

But there's another way.

Salvation changes your story. When you receive Jesus—the moment of salvation —you are no longer destined for that second death. You may still experience the first one—but you will rise again to **eternal life**. Life with God. Life without end. No fear. No pain. No separation. Just forever with the One who loves you more than you can imagine.

You don't have to die twice.
You can live once—**truly live**—forever.

> *"But the cowardly, the unbelieving, the vile... their place will be in the fiery lake of burning sulfur. This is the second death."*
>
> —Revelation 21:8 (NIV)

> *"Very truly I tell you, whoever hears my word and believes him who sent me has eternal life and will not be judged but has crossed over from death to life."*
>
> —John 5:24 (NIV)

✦ You Can't Fix Sin on Your Own

No amount of good works can clean the stain of sin. You can't earn forgiveness by trying harder, doing better, or pretending you've never fallen short. Sin isn't just about actions—it's about a condition of the heart that only God can heal.

Only one thing can restore what was broken: the righteousness of Christ.

Jesus didn't come to make bad people behave better—He came to make dead people alive. When you receive Him—the moment you placed your faith in Him, your sins are not just forgiven—they're exchanged. He takes your sin and gives you His righteousness.

You don't work for salvation. You receive it by faith—and then begin living from it, clothed in Christ's perfection, not your performance.

> *"For He made Him who knew no sin to be sin for us, that we might become the righteousness of God in Him."*
>
> —2 Corinthians 5:21 (NKJV)

📚 For Further Reading

- **Genesis 3**—The first sin and its consequences
- **Romans 6:23**—The cost of sin and the gift of salvation
- **Revelation 21:8**—The second death
- **2 Corinthians 5:17–21**—Righteousness through Christ
- **Romans 8:14–16**—Led by the Spirit and called God's children
- **Galatians 4:6–7**—You are no longer a slave, but a child and heir
- **John 14:16–17**—The Holy Spirit will live in you and never leave
- **Romans 3:23**—We have all sinned
- **Ephesians 2:8–9**—Salvation is a gift, not something we earn
- **1 John 4:15**—Confessing Jesus as the Son of God brings His presence into you
- **John 3:3–7, 16**—Jesus explains the necessity of being "born again"
- **Hebrews 7:25**—Jesus is always interceding for those who come to God through Him

📖 Reflection Questions

1. What part of the salvation story surprised or impacted you the most?
   (Was it something about the fall, the cost Jesus paid, or the way God invites you back?)

2. How would you describe your relationship with God right now?
   (Is it distant? Growing? Brand new? Honest?)

3. What evidence do you see in your life that points to real transformation?
   (Even if it's small—what's different since you chose to believe?)

2.

Walking in Righteousness

✦ A New Way to Live

Salvation isn't just about being saved from something—it's also about being saved **for** something.

When you receive Christ, you're not only forgiven—you're invited to walk in a new way of living: a life that reflects who God is and what He's done in you. That way of life is called **righteousness**.

✦ What is Righteousness?

Righteousness means being in **right standing with God**—and then choosing to live in alignment with that truth. It doesn't mean being perfect. It means belonging to the One who is perfect, and letting Him shape your thoughts, decisions, and desires.

Through Jesus, you've been made righteous before God. That's your **position**. But walking in righteousness is your **practice**—your daily response to the grace you've received.

> *"For He made Him who knew no sin to be sin for us, that we might become the righteousness of God in Him."*
>
> —2 Corinthians 5:21 (NKJV)

✦ Righteousness is a Relationship

You don't walk in righteousness by following rules—you do it by following Jesus. It's a relationship, not a performance.

Jesus calls us to live with **childlike faith**—to trust Him, obey Him, and stay close even when we don't have it all figured out.

> *"Unless you are converted and become as little children, you will by no means enter the Kingdom of heaven."*
>
> —Matthew 18:3–4 (NKJV)

✦ From Slaves to Servants

Before salvation, sin ruled over you like a cruel master. Whether you recognized it or not, you were under its control. Sin isn't just bad behavior—it's a condition of the heart. It shapes how you think, how you treat others, and how you see yourself and God. It traps you in cycles of guilt, pride, addiction, fear, selfishness, shame, and brokenness. You didn't really have a choice.

But Jesus broke the power of that master.

When you received salvation, you were set free—not just from the penalty of sin, but from its grip on your daily life. That freedom doesn't mean doing whatever you want. It means for the first time, you actually can choose to do what's right. You've been rescued to live with purpose, not pressure—to walk in truth, not torment—to serve a loving God instead of a ruthless enemy.

You're not just forgiven. You're free.

> *"For sin shall not have dominion over you, for you are not under law but under grace."*
>
> —Romans 6:14 (NKJV)

✦ The Process of Righteous Living

Salvation is the starting point—but living a righteous life is a daily walk. God doesn't expect perfection, but He does invite participation. As you grow in your faith, there's a simple pattern that will help you stay close to Him and walk in freedom. It's not about following rules—it's about responding to His love.

1. **Confess your sin.** God already knows. But confession breaks the power of shame and invites His healing. It also helps you face your past choices, so they're no longer hidden —even if it's just from yourself. Confession loosens sin's grip and destroys one of its most powerful weapons: secrecy.
2. **Repent.** Repentance isn't just feeling guilty or sorry—it's choosing a new direction. It means turning away from what once held you back and moving toward God with intention. True repentance is more than emotion—it's transformation. It says, "I don't want to live like that anymore," and then takes the steps, however small, to live differently. It's the beginning of a new story.
3. **Make a new choice.** Righteousness is not about perfection—it's about consistent direction. Every new day gives you opportunities to choose differently. With God's help, you can reject the patterns that once defined you and walk in freedom—one decision at a time. Even when it's hard, obedience leads to peace. And each right choice makes the next one easier.

"Do not let sin reign in your mortal body... but present yourselves to God as being alive from the dead."

—Romans 6:12–13 (NKJV)

📚 For Further Reading

- **2 Corinthians 5:21**—You have been made righteous in Christ
- **Matthew 18:3–4**—Childlike faith and trust
- **Romans 6:6–14**—Freedom from slavery to sin
- **Psalm 32:5**—Confession brings forgiveness
- **1 John 1:9**—God is faithful to forgive and cleanse

Reflection Questions

1. How has your view of righteousness changed since reading this chapter? (Is it more about relationship than you previously thought?)

2. What area of your life is God inviting you to walk in greater alignment with Him?

3. When have you experienced God's grace helping you make a new choice?

3.
Transformation

✦ Salvation Isn't the End—It's the Beginning

The moment you accept salvation, something changes. But that moment is only the starting point. Salvation launches a lifelong journey—a process of becoming more and more like Jesus. That process is called **transformation**.

God doesn't just rescue you from something—He invites you to become someone. Not a new version of who others expect you to be, but the person He originally designed you to be before sin, shame, or struggle ever took hold.

✦ What Does It Mean to Be Transformed?

To be transformed means to be completely changed in form, character, and direction. It's deeper than behavior modification. It's not about fixing yourself—it's about surrendering yourself so God can do the work from the inside out.

✦ You Become a Representative of Christ

Salvation doesn't just change your destination—it changes your identity. You become an ambassador of Christ, carrying His presence into everyday life. The way you speak, love, respond, forgive, and live is now a living testimony to the One who saved you. People may not read the Bible, but they will read you.

You don't just talk about Jesus—you reflect Him. That's why your character matters. You represent His Kingdom with every interaction. As His representative, you bring light to dark places, hope to weary hearts, and truth to a confused world.

This isn't about perfection—it's about presence. The Holy Spirit within you makes it possible to live a life that points people to Christ.

> *"Now then, we are ambassadors for Christ... for He made Him who knew no sin to be sin for us, that we might become the righteousness of God in Him."*
>
> —2 Corinthians 5:20–21 (NKJV)

✦ You Are Empowered to Love Unconditionally

Most love in this world comes with conditions—I'll love you if… or as long as you… But the love God offers is different. It's not based on how good you are, how much you give, or whether you've earned it. His love is steady, sacrificial, and unshakable—even when you mess up.

And when Christ lives in you, that kind of love begins to grow inside your heart too. Suddenly, you can forgive when it doesn't make sense. You can be kind when others are cruel. You can show compassion without expecting anything in return. Not because it's easy—but because the Spirit of God is empowering you.

You don't have to manufacture this love. You just have to receive it—and let it overflow.

> *"For God so loved the world that He gave His only begotten Son…"*
>
> —John 3:16 (KJV)

✦ You Get a Fresh Start

You're not just forgiven—you're made new. Salvation isn't a bandage over your past; it's a complete rebirth. In Christ, you don't carry around the old labels of shame, failure, or regret. Your identity is no longer rooted in who you were or what you did—it's grounded in who Jesus is and what He has done for you.

You may still remember your past, but it no longer defines your future. The old you was buried, and a new you has been raised to life. You have been spiritually reborn—not by human effort, but by the power of God's Word and His Spirit.

Every day is a new opportunity to live in that truth—to walk in freedom, grow in grace, and embrace the person God is shaping you to be.

> *"Being born again, not of corruptible seed but incorruptible, through the word of God which lives and abides forever."*
>
> —1 Peter 1:23 (NKJV)

✦ You Are Set Free from Condemnation

God doesn't shame you when you mess up—and you will mess up. He draws you back with love. Through Christ, you are no longer defined by your worst moments or past failures. Condemnation tries to convince you that you'll never change, that you're hopeless, or too far gone—worthless. But that's not the voice of God.

Conviction, on the other hand, is the Holy Spirit gently showing you what needs to shift—not to shame you, but to heal you. He corrects you like a loving Father who wants to protect you and restore your peace.

When you belong to Jesus, the weight of guilt no longer has permission to rule your life. You can breathe easier. Walk lighter. Stand taller. You are fully seen, fully loved, and fully forgiven.

> *"There is therefore now no condemnation to those who are in Christ Jesus, who do not walk according to the flesh but according to the Spirit."*
>
> —Romans 8:1 (NKJV)

You've learned what salvation makes possible—freedom, forgiveness, a fresh start, and a new identity in Christ. But how does it all work? What exactly is salvation, and why do we need it in the first place? In the next chapter, we'll slow down and take a deeper look at what salvation truly means—so you can understand the beauty, the cost, and the power of what Jesus has done for you.

📚 For Further Reading

- **2 Corinthians 5:20–21**—We are Christ's ambassadors
- **John 3:16**—Love that transforms
- **1 Peter 1:23**—Born again by the living Word
- **Romans 8:1**—No condemnation in Christ
- **Titus 3:5**—We are saved through the washing of rebirth

📖 Reflection Questions

1. What parts of your life have already started to change since receiving salvation?
   (Think of small shifts—desires, mindset, relationships.)

2. What does "transformation" mean to you personally?

3. Is there an area of your life where you sense God inviting you to grow or let go?

4.
Understanding Salvation

✦ Salvation Affects Every Part of You

When you receive salvation, it's not just your spirit that changes. Salvation touches every part of who you are—spirit, soul, and body. God designed you as a whole person, and His work in you is complete and transformational.

You're not just a spiritual being. You also have thoughts, emotions, memories, physical experiences—and God wants to redeem it all.

✦ Spirit, Soul, and Body

You may have heard it said: *"You are a spirit, you have a soul, and you live in a body."* But what does that actually mean?

Let's break it down:

- Your spirit is the deepest part of who you are. It's the eternal part of you—the part God designed to connect with Him. When God created

Adam, He breathed His own breath into him, and Adam became a living being. That divine breath is what makes your spirit alive. Before salvation, your spirit is disconnected from God and spiritually "asleep." But the moment you receive Christ, your spirit is made alive again—fully awakened and reconnected to your Creator.

- Your soul is made up of your mind, will, and emotions. It's how you think, feel, and make choices. Your soul is where you experience joy and sorrow, anger and peace, confidence and fear. Before salvation, your soul tends to be in charge—making decisions based on your feelings, circumstances, and human reasoning. But after salvation, your soul begins a process of restoration as it comes under the influence of your renewed spirit and the truth of God's Word.
- Your body is your physical self. It's the part of you that eats, sleeps, hurts, heals, walks, talks, and interacts with the world. It responds to what's going on in your spirit and soul. When your spirit and soul are aligned with God, your body often reflects it—through peace, energy, and purpose. But when you're emotionally broken or spiritually disconnected, your body can carry the weight of that, too.

Salvation isn't just a moment—it's a movement. It awakens your spirit, begins healing your soul, and eventually impacts how you live in your body. And while these three parts are distinct, they're also deeply connected. What affects one part of you can influence the others. That's why walking with Jesus is about becoming whole—not just spiritually, but emotionally and physically too.

Let's take a closer look at how salvation transforms each part of who you are.

✦ Salvation of the Spirit → Justification

This is the part of salvation that happens **instantly**. The moment you receive Christ, something powerful takes place in your spirit—you are made righteous before God. That doesn't mean you suddenly become perfect in your behavior. It means your standing before God is changed forever.

Where there was once separation, there is now connection. Where there was guilt, there is now grace.

Justification is a legal term. Imagine standing in a courtroom, fully aware of the charges against you. But just as the sentence is about to be read, Jesus steps in and says, "I'll take it." The Judge slams the gavel down and declares, "Not guilty."

That's justification.

It means God no longer sees your sin—He sees Christ's righteousness covering you.

> *"He has removed our sins as far from us as the east is from the west."*
>
> —Psalm 103:12 (NLT)

> *"Being justified freely by His grace through the redemption that is in Christ Jesus."*
>
> —Romans 3:24 (KJV)

This doesn't mean you'll never sin again, but it does mean that sin no longer defines you. When you do fall short, you now have the power to confess, turn, and receive forgiveness without shame or fear. You don't lose your salvation every time you stumble—your salvation is secured in Christ.

But be careful not to treat grace like a permission slip to do whatever you want. Paul addresses this in Romans 6:

> *"Shall we continue in sin, that grace may abound? God forbid."*
>
> —(Romans 6:1–2, KJV paraphrased)

Justification is not something you earn. You can't work hard enough, be good enough, or clean yourself up enough to deserve it. It is a gift of grace that comes through faith in Jesus.

> *"Therefore, as by the offense of one judgment came upon all men to condemnation; even so by the righteousness of One the free gift came upon all men unto justification of life."*
>
> —Romans 5:18 (KJV)

At the moment of justification:

- Your sins are forgiven.
- Your spirit is made alive.
- You are born again into the family of God.

You are given a new nature—a divine nature empowered by the Holy Spirit.

> *"I will give you a new heart and put a new spirit within you."*
>
> —Ezekiel 36:26 (NLT)

This is where the journey begins. You've been made right with God. You are no longer a slave to sin. You are justified—just as if you'd never sinned.

✦ Salvation of the Soul → Sanctification

This part takes time. Sanctification is the ongoing process of being made holy—set apart for God's purposes. It's not about being perfect. It's about choosing daily to let the Holy Spirit shape your thoughts, actions, and desires so they reflect the character of Jesus.

> *"Be transformed by the renewing of your mind..."*
>
> —Romans 12:2 (NKJV)

> *"Put off the old self... be made new in the attitude of your minds."*
>
> —Ephesians 4:22–23 (NIV)

Before salvation, your soul—your mind, will, and emotions—called the shots. You were driven by what felt good, what seemed right, or what others expected.

But now, as a believer, your soul comes under new leadership. God begins to renew your mind, reshape your desires, and restore your emotional life.

That doesn't happen overnight. Sanctification is progressive—a journey, not a destination. Each day, you will face many choices like these:

- Will I respond with kindness or lash out in anger?
- Will I gossip or stay silent?
- Will I choose bitterness or forgiveness?

These daily decisions are where sanctification happens.

> *"This day I call the heavens and the earth as witnesses... I have set before you life and death, blessings and curses. Now choose life..."*
>
> —Deuteronomy 30:19 (NIV)

Sanctification is also the separation from the seduction of sin. Sin is sneaky. It whispers in ways that seem harmless—just one lie, one click, one grudge.

But the Holy Spirit helps you recognize those traps and choose a better way. You are not powerless. You can "put off the old self" and live differently.

> *"Mortify therefore your members which are upon the earth... put off all these: anger, wrath, malice, blasphemy... and put on the new man..."*
>
> —Colossians 3:5–10 (KJV)

This transformation isn't something you have to figure out alone. The Holy Spirit lives in you to guide, empower, and strengthen you. But it still requires your participation.

> *"Work out your salvation with fear and trembling..."*
>
> —Philippians 2:12 (NASB)

As you cooperate with God, your soul is renewed, your choices begin to align with His will, and your life starts to bear fruit. This is sanctification. It's the day-by-day reality of learning to live like someone who belongs to Jesus.

✦ Salvation of the Body → Glorification

This part is still to come. It's the final step in your salvation journey—one that will take place in the future when Christ returns.

Glorification is when God removes every last trace of sin—not just from your spirit or your soul, but from your physical body. You'll be completely transformed, inside and out.

Right now, we live in human bodies that age, get sick, and are affected by the brokenness of this world. But one day, when the last trumpet sounds, everything will change.

Your mortal body—the one that feels pain, gets tired, and wrestles with temptation—will be exchanged for an eternal, incorruptible body. A new body. One fit for the presence of God.

> *"It is sown a natural body, it is raised a spiritual body. There is a natural body, and there is a spiritual body."*
>
> —1 Corinthians 15:44 (KJV)

> *"We will all be changed—in a moment, in the twinkling of an eye... the mortal will put on immortality."*
>
> —1 Corinthians 15:51–53 (NLT)

> *"He will transform our lowly body to be like His glorious body..."*
>
> —Philippians 3:21 (ESV)

Glorification is God's final act of redemption. It's when salvation reaches its full expression—not just spiritually and emotionally, but physically. You'll no longer struggle with sin. You'll no longer experience weakness. No sickness. No more death. No more aching body or emotional wounds carried in your cells. It will all be gone.

You will live forever in the presence of God—completely whole, completely pure, and completely free.

That's what we're moving toward. That's the promise of glorification. And it's worth waiting for.

✦ Quick Snapshot

Justification happens the moment you receive salvation. In that instant, your spirit is redeemed. You are made right with God—not because of what you've done, but because of what Jesus has done for you. This is a finished, permanent reality. You are no longer guilty before God; you are justified by grace.

Sanctification is the ongoing process that follows. It affects your soul—your mind, will, and emotions. Day by day, God renews your thinking, heals your heart, and reshapes your desires. This transformation doesn't happen overnight, but steadily over time as you walk with Him. You are being changed from the inside out.

Glorification is the future promise of salvation, when your body will be fully restored. One day, when Jesus returns, everything broken by sin—including sickness, aging, and death—will be completely made new. This is the final completion of salvation, when you will be perfected in eternity.

Salvation touches your spirit immediately, your soul continually, and your body ultimately. It is a finished work, an ongoing transformation, and a future hope—all wrapped together in God's redemptive plan.

Now that you've seen how salvation affects every part of who you are, it's time to look at the foundation that makes all of this possible. Salvation isn't something we earn—it's something Jesus accomplished.

In the next chapter, we'll explore what Christ actually did for you on the cross and why His finished work changes everything.

📚 For Further Reading

- **Romans 3:24**—Justified by grace
- **Psalm 103:12**—Sins removed far from us
- **Romans 12:2**—Transformation through renewed thinking
- **Ephesians 4:22–24**—Putting off the old self
- **1 Corinthians 15:51–53**—The promise of glorification
- **Philippians 3:21**—A new, glorified body

📝 Reflection Questions

1. Which part of salvation—spirit, soul, or body—feels most relevant to you right now? Why?

2. How have you noticed God renewing your thinking or healing your emotions?

3. What does the promise of glorification (a renewed, eternal body) mean to you personally?

5.
The Finished Work of Christ

✦ It is Finished—But Not Over

When Jesus said, *"It is finished,"* from the cross (John 19:30 KJV), He wasn't just marking the end of His suffering—He was declaring the completion of His mission.

The work of salvation was done. The price had been paid. The way had been opened.

But that wasn't the end of the story. It was the beginning of new life for anyone who believes.

✦ What Did Jesus Finish?

The cross was not an accident—it was the plan. Jesus came with one mission: to make a way for us to be reconciled to the Father. That mission was accomplished through His perfect life, sacrificial death, and victorious resurrection.

✦ Atonement: Making Things Right Again

To atone means to cover, to reconcile, to make things right between two separated parties. In the context of salvation, it means restoring the broken relationship between humanity and God—a relationship fractured by sin.

From the moment Adam and Eve disobeyed God in the garden, that fracture extended to all of us. Humanity was sold into the bondage of sin, and the price to be bought back was unimaginably high.

According to God's justice, only innocent, sinless blood could pay that debt. Jesus—the perfect, sinless Son of God—willingly became that payment.

He didn't just sympathize with our brokenness—He stepped into it. He became our High Priest, offering not the blood of animals like in the Old Testament, but His own blood.

His sacrifice fulfilled the legal requirement for redemption and tore down the barrier between God and man.

Through His atonement, Jesus built a bridge.

He paid the penalty of sin and made a way for you to walk freely into relationship with Father, Son, and Holy Spirit—no longer bound by guilt, shame, or separation.

> *"We also rejoice in God through our Lord Jesus Christ, through whom we have now received the atonement."*
>
> —Romans 5:11 (AKJV)

> *"For it pleased the Father that in Him all the fullness should dwell, and by Him to reconcile all things to Himself... having made peace through the blood of His cross."*
>
> —Colossians 1:19–20 (NKJV)

Because of Jesus, you are no longer cut off. You are no longer a slave to sin. You've been bought back—with love, with blood, and with purpose.

✦ Redemption: You Were Bought Back

Redemption means to purchase something back, to rescue or reclaim what was lost or held captive.

It's a powerful word—one that speaks of both value and victory. You don't redeem something worthless. You redeem what matters.

From the moment sin entered the world, humanity became trapped—enslaved by darkness, shame, and spiritual death.

But God saw your worth. He didn't leave you there. He paid the highest possible price to bring you back to Himself.

That price wasn't silver or gold. It wasn't a temporary payment. It was the life and blood of Jesus—the perfect Lamb without blemish or defect.

> *"You were not redeemed with corruptible things… but with the precious blood of Christ, as of a lamb without blemish and without spot."*
>
> —1 Peter 1:18–19 (AKJV)

✦ Propitiation: God's Justice Satisfied

God is perfectly holy—and because He is holy, He is also just. That means He can't overlook sin or pretend it doesn't matter. Justice requires a payment for wrongdoing.

And left to ourselves, that payment would fall on us. But here's the good news: Jesus stepped in and took our place.

That's what propitiation means. It's a big word with a beautiful truth. Jesus satisfied the just wrath of God—not by avoiding it, but by absorbing it.

On the cross, He bore the full weight of sin's judgment so that we wouldn't have to. He stood between us and the penalty we deserved and made peace possible.

> *"God presented Christ as a propitiation through the shedding of His blood, to be received by faith. He did this to demonstrate His righteousness..."*
>
> —Romans 3:25 (paraphrased from NKJV)

This wasn't divine punishment—it was divine love in action. Jesus didn't die because God was angry. He died because God loved you too much to leave you separated and condemned.

Propitiation means the price has been paid, the wrath has been turned away, and mercy now flows freely. Because of Jesus, you don't have to fear judgment. You are invited into grace.

✦ Reconciliation: Relationship Restored

Sin didn't just break a rule—it broke a relationship. It created distance between us and the God who made us, a separation so deep that no amount of good behavior could bridge it.

But Jesus did.

Through His sacrifice, Jesus didn't just remove our guilt—He removed the barrier that kept us apart from God. That's what reconciliation means: a broken relationship made whole again.

We are no longer enemies of God or strangers to His love. We are welcomed back, not as visitors—but as sons and daughters.

> *"God... reconciled us to Himself through Jesus Christ... not counting our sins against us."*
>
> —2 Corinthians 5:18–19 (NKJV)

Reconciliation is more than forgiveness—it's friendship restored. You don't have to stand at a distance, hoping God still wants you. He does.

In Christ, you are fully known, fully accepted, and fully invited into His presence. You belong in the family. You are wanted here.

✦ Repentance as a Lifestyle

Reconciliation isn't the end of the story—it's the beginning of a restored relationship that stays alive through repentance. The same grace that brought you back to God keeps drawing you closer day by day.

Repentance isn't just the doorway into salvation—it's the pathway of a surrendered life. When Jesus paid the price for sin, He didn't just make forgiveness possible; He made transformation possible.

Every time we turn from old ways of thinking and return to God's truth, we're living out the power of the cross.

To repent means "to change your mind." It's not about shame or self-punishment—it's about realignment.

It's learning to see sin the way God sees it and choosing again to walk in His ways. The more we know His love, the quicker we are to turn back when we drift.

Repentance isn't a one-time event; it's a rhythm of grace. Each day, the Holy Spirit gently reveals attitudes or habits that don't reflect who we are in Christ. When we respond with humility and obedience, we grow stronger in freedom.

"If we confess our sins, He is faithful and just to forgive us our sins and to cleanse us from all unrighteousness."

—1 John 1:9 (NKJV)

Repentance keeps the heart tender. It keeps us close. It reminds us that holiness isn't a performance—it's partnership. The same grace that saved us continues to transform us, one turning-back moment at a time.

📖 For Further Reading

- **John 19:30**—It is finished
- **Romans 5:11**—Atonement through Christ
- **1 Peter 1:18–19**—Redeemed by His blood
- **Romans 3:25–26**—Propitiation and righteousness
- **2 Corinthians 5:18–21**—Reconciliation through Christ

✝ Reflection Questions

1. Which part of Christ's finished work feels most personal to you right now—atonement, redemption, propitiation, or reconciliation? Why?

2. What does it mean to you that Jesus said, *"It is finished"*?

3. How does knowing you've been bought back and reconciled affect the way you approach God?

6.

You Are an Eternal Being

✦ You Were Made for More Than This Life

You are not just a physical body. You are an eternal being—created to live forever. While your body will one day stop breathing, your spirit and soul will not die. They continue on, beyond this life, into eternity.

And there are only two destinations: eternity with God, or eternal separation from Him.

That's why salvation matters. It's not just about living a better life now—it's about securing your eternal home. Jesus made the way back to the Father so that eternal life could be yours.

When you receive salvation, you're not just saved **from** something—you're saved **for** something: everlasting life in God's presence, where there is no more pain, fear, or separation.

> *"And this is the testimony: that God has given us eternal life, and this life is in His Son. He who has the Son has life; he who does not have the Son of God does not have life."*
>
> —1 John 5:11–12 (NKJV)

This truth shifts everything. It means your choices matter. Your relationship with God matters. And it means this life isn't all there is. Eternity is real—and God wants to spend it with you.

✦ What Is Eternity?

Eternity isn't just a really long time. It's a completely different kind of existence—beyond time, beyond clocks and calendars. You don't measure eternity in years or minutes. You live it—fully aware, fully present, and either fully with God or fully separated from Him.

There are only two eternal outcomes as previously noted:

- Eternal life with God
- Eternal separation from God

And here's where it gets beautiful: eternal life doesn't begin after you die—it begins the moment you receive Jesus. That's when your spirit is made alive and your forever with God begins.

> *"And this is eternal life: that they may know You, the only true God, and Jesus Christ whom You have sent."*
>
> —John 17:3 (NKJV)

You don't have to wait for heaven to experience eternal life. When you say yes to Jesus, eternity starts now—with relationship, with purpose, and with the security of knowing where you're going.

✦ Death Isn't the End—It's a Transition

The world sees death as the final stop. But for believers, it's a doorway into something far greater.

Jesus defeated death so you could live again—not just spiritually, but physically in a glorified, eternal body.

> *"I give them eternal life, and they shall never perish; neither shall anyone snatch them out of My hand."*
>
> —John 10:28 (NKJV)

✦ You Get to Choose Where You'll Spend Eternity

God doesn't force anyone into relationship with Him. He invites. He offers. And He waits for your response.

Those who accept salvation will spend eternity **with Him** in perfect peace and joy. Those who reject Him will remain separated forever. This isn't about punishment—it's about the consequences of refusing the only path to life.

> *"He who believes in the Son has everlasting life; and he who does not believe the Son shall not see life."*
>
> —John 3:36 (KJV)

✦ Eternity Starts Now

Eternal life isn't something you wait for—it's something you begin walking in the moment you're saved. You get to know God. Hear His voice. Live in His presence. Right now.

> *"God has given us eternal life, and this life is in His Son."*
>
> —1 John 5:11 (NKJV)

You were created to live forever—with purpose, with peace, and with God.

📚 For Further Reading

- **John 17:3**—Eternal life is knowing God
- **John 10:28**—Eternal security in Christ
- **John 3:36**—Two eternal paths
- **1 John 5:11**—Eternal life is found in Jesus
- **Ecclesiastes 3:11**—God placed eternity in our hearts

📖 Reflection Questions

1. How does knowing you're an eternal being change how you think about this life?

2. When you think of eternity, what emotions or questions rise up?

3. What does it mean to you that eternal life begins the moment you know Jesus—not just after you die?

7.

Confession of Faith

✦ The Most Important Decision You'll Ever Make

Salvation isn't about joining a religion—it's about entering a relationship.

God loves you. He's been pursuing your heart all along. And if you've read this far, maybe something inside you knows it's time.

Whether you're saying yes to Jesus for the first time or returning after a long journey, this is your moment. Don't wait for perfect timing or perfect faith—God simply wants a willing heart.

> *"If you confess with your mouth the Lord Jesus and believe in your heart that God has raised Him from the dead, you will be saved."*
>
> —Romans 10:9 (NKJV)

✦ A Prayer of Salvation

You can use this prayer as a guide. The words are not magic—it's your heart that matters. Speak it aloud or whisper it quietly. God hears you.

Lord, I come to You in the name of Jesus.

I confess that I am a sinner in need of grace. I believe that Jesus Christ is the Son of God, that He died for my sins, and that He rose from the dead. I accept Him as my Savior and declare Him as Lord of my life.

Please forgive me, cleanse me, and make me new. Fill me with Your Holy Spirit and teach me how to walk with You every day.

From this moment on, I belong to You.
Thank You for saving me. Thank You for loving me.
Thank You for giving me eternal life.

In Jesus' name,
Amen.

✦ Water Baptism: An Outward Declaration of an Inward Change

Water baptism is more than a ceremony. It's an act of obedience—a public declaration that you belong to Jesus. When you are baptized, you're saying to the world, *"My life has been changed."*

Baptism doesn't save you—Jesus already did that. But it's an outward picture of what has already happened inside you. Going down into the water symbolizes being buried with Christ; coming up out of the water represents being raised to new life with Him.

> *"Or do you not know that as many of us as were baptized into Christ Jesus were baptized into His death? Therefore we were buried with Him through baptism into death, that just as Christ was raised from the dead by the glory of the Father, even so we also should walk in newness of life."*
>
> —Romans 6:3–4 (NKJV)

Baptism is your first step of faith after salvation—your first opportunity to say, *"I belong to Jesus, and I'm not turning back."* It's a moment of joy, commitment, and identity.

If you've given your life to Christ but haven't yet been baptized, pray about taking this step. Talk to a pastor or church leader. You don't need to have everything figured out—you just need to be willing to follow.

> *"Repent, and let every one of you be baptized in the name of Jesus Christ for the remission of sins; and you shall receive the gift of the Holy Spirit."*
>
> —Acts 2:38 (NKJV)

Baptism doesn't make you perfect, but it does mark you as His. It's your way of saying, *"The old me is gone, and I'm walking in new life."*

✦ What Happens Next?

If you prayed that prayer with sincerity, heaven is celebrating—and so am I. Your past is covered. Your spirit is reborn. And your journey with God has truly begun.

You may not feel different right away, but trust that something has shifted. And as you walk forward, chapter by chapter, you'll begin to see that the God who saved you also walks with you—day by day, step by step.

📚 For Further Reading

- **Romans 10:9–10**—Confess and believe for salvation
- **John 1:12**—You are now a child of God
- **2 Corinthians 5:17**—You are a new creation
- **Luke 15:7**—Heaven rejoices over one who turns to God
- **Ephesians 2:8–9**—Salvation is a gift, not something you earn

Reflection Questions

1. What did it feel like to speak those words of confession and faith out loud?

2. What do you hope will begin to change in your life as you walk with God?

3. Who could you tell about your decision—or ask to walk with you as you grow?

8.

Tools to Help You Walk Out Your Salvation

✦ Salvation Is a Starting Line—Not a Finish Line

Saying yes to Jesus is the beginning of a new life, but walking it out day by day takes intention. Just like a seed needs water and light to grow, your relationship with God needs regular nourishment.

Thankfully, God has given us tools—practices that help us grow strong, stay rooted in truth, and experience His presence in everyday life.

Here are some tools to assist you on your journey. Each one is introduced briefly here, but don't worry—we'll explore them in greater detail throughout the rest of the book.

As you keep reading, you'll learn how to use these tools with confidence and clarity.

✦ Read the Word

The Bible is more than a book—it's a lifeline. It tells you who God is, what He's done, and who you are in Him. Reading the Word builds your faith and renews your mind.

> *"Oh, how I love Your law! It is my meditation all the day."*
>
> —Psalm 119:97 (NKJV)

> *"All Scripture is inspired by God and is useful to teach us what is true... God uses it to prepare and equip His people to do every good work."*
>
> —2 Timothy 3:16–17 (NLT)

✦ Talk to God in Prayer

Prayer is not a formula—it's a conversation. It's how you build a relationship with God. You don't have to sound perfect or use fancy words. Just talk to Him. He's listening.

> *"Pray without ceasing."*
>
> —1 Thessalonians 5:17 (KJV)

> *"May my meditation be sweet to Him; I will be glad in the Lord."*
>
> —Psalm 104:34 (NKJV)

✦ Spend Time with Other Believers—The Power of Connection

Salvation is personal, but it's not meant to be private. From the very beginning, God designed His people to grow in community. You were never meant to walk out your faith alone.

When you join a local church or small group, you're stepping into the spiritual family God created for you. It's where you'll be encouraged, strengthened, and reminded of truth when life gets hard.

It's also where your gifts begin to grow—because spiritual maturity happens in relationship.

> *"And let us consider one another to provoke unto love and to good works: not forsaking the assembling of ourselves together... but exhorting one another."*
>
> —Hebrews 10:24–25 (KJV)

Community keeps your roots deep. It reminds you that you're part of something bigger—the Body of Christ. Every believer needs connection, accountability, and encouragement.

As you worship, learn, and serve alongside others, you'll find that your faith grows stronger than it ever could in isolation.

You're not just called to believe. You're called to belong.

✦ Do Good Works (Because You're Saved—Not to Be Saved)

You don't earn salvation by doing good things, but once you've been changed by Christ, good works naturally flow out of that transformation. You become a light to others.

> *"Let your light so shine before men, that they may see your good works and glorify your Father in heaven."*
>
> —Matthew 5:16 (NKJV)

✦ Stay Connected to the Source

There will be moments when you feel dry or distracted—but don't disconnect. Keep showing up. Keep praying. Keep listening.

Transformation happens over time, not overnight. God isn't looking for perfection—He's looking for people who will walk with Him, even when it's hard. That's what it means to walk out your salvation.

> *"He who began a good work in you will carry it on to completion..."*
>
> —Philippians 1:6 (NIV)

📚 For Further Reading

- **Psalm 119:97**—Love for God's Word
- **2 Timothy 3:16–17**—Scripture equips you
- **1 Thessalonians 5:17**—Stay in communication with God
- **Hebrews 10:25**—The power of gathering
- **Matthew 5:16**—Let your light shine
- **Philippians 1:6**—He's not finished with you

📖 Reflection Questions

1. Which tool—Word, prayer, community, or good works—do you already use regularly? Which one feels new or unfamiliar?

2. What small, daily step could help you grow deeper in your walk with Jesus?

3. Who can you ask to walk alongside you for encouragement, prayer, or accountability?

9.
Stepping Stones

10 Truths to Carry With You

✦ You've Started Something Sacred.

Walking in salvation isn't a single decision—it's a daily journey. Every step matters. Every moment builds on the one before it. And when the path feels uncertain, these truths are your stepping stones. Let them remind you who you are, what's been done for you, and where you're going.

1. Everyone is born into sin—but no one is beyond redemption.

You didn't choose to be born into a broken world, but you can choose to be born again.

2. Salvation means being rescued from sin and reunited with God.

It's not just deliverance from death—it's a return to relationship.

3. When you're saved, you become a new creation.

You are not who you were. You are not what you've done. You are His.

4. Confession and repentance open the door to transformation.

You don't have to carry shame. You're invited into freedom.

5. You are justified, sanctified, and one day will be glorified.

This is a spiritual reality, a daily process, and a future promise.

6. Jesus paid the full price for your salvation.

You don't have to earn what He already finished.

7. Salvation includes redemption, reconciliation, and peace with God.

You've been bought back. You've been brought close. You are at peace.

8. You have the power to walk in righteousness.

Sin no longer defines you or controls you.

9. Your life is eternal—and eternity has already begun.

You're not waiting for something someday. You're living it now.

10. You're not walking alone.

The Holy Spirit is with you. The Word is your guide. God calls you His.

> *"He who began a good work in you will carry it on to completion until the day of Christ Jesus."*
>
> —Philippians 1:6 (NIV)

✦ Key Terms to Remember

These words will appear throughout the pages ahead. Take a moment to read them slowly and let their meaning settle in your heart. Each one describes a part of the beautiful story God is writing in you.

Salvation—God's rescue and restoration plan. Through faith in Jesus, you are forgiven, made new, and brought back into relationship with Him.

Born Again—A fresh beginning. When you receive Christ, your spirit is reborn and you start a brand-new life with God.

Redemption—To be bought back. Jesus paid the price for your freedom and restored what sin once stole.

Justification—To be declared righteous before God. The moment you believe, you are made right with Him—as if you had never sinned.

Sanctification—The ongoing process of becoming more like Jesus. The Holy Spirit renews your heart, mind, and character day by day.

Glorification—The final stage of salvation. One day you will see Jesus face-to-face, completely whole and free from every trace of sin.

Grace—God's undeserved kindness and power at work in your life. Grace saves you, teaches you, and strengthens you to live in freedom.

Faith—Trusting God enough to take Him at His Word and act on it—even when you can't yet see the outcome.

Repentance—Turning away from sin and toward God. It's not punishment; it's a change of direction that keeps your heart aligned with His.

The Church—The family of believers. Every follower of Jesus belongs to His Body, called to grow, worship, and serve together.

→ What Comes Next

You've taken the first steps of salvation—but this journey doesn't end here. Salvation is the beginning of a new life, not the finish line.

In the chapters ahead, the focus will shift from what was done for you to who now walks with you. God never intended you to navigate growth, healing, or transformation on your own. From the moment you believed, He placed His Spirit within you—to guide you, strengthen you, and help you live out what salvation made possible.

The Holy Spirit is not distant or abstract. He is present, personal, and active in your everyday life. He teaches you truth, reminds you of God's promises, and empowers you to walk in freedom—step by step.

As you move forward, you're not being asked to strive harder or do better on your own. You're invited to learn how to walk in partnership with the Spirit—listening, responding, and growing over time.

This is where the journey deepens. And you won't walk it alone.

> *"Lord, thank You for saving me. Help me to walk in the truth that I am Yours, justified by grace, and empowered to live a new life."*

PART II

Lord, I Need Help!

Walking With the Holy Spirit

"And I will ask the Father, and He will give you another Helper, that He may be with you forever."

—John 14:16 (NASB)

🎯 Objective

This section will help you understand who the Holy Spirit is and how He works in the life of a believer. You'll discover that the Holy Spirit isn't a distant mystery, but a present Helper—your Comforter, Guide, and Source of power for everyday living. This part will equip you to hear His voice, walk in obedience, and rely on His presence as you grow in faith.

---- ◆ ----

📖 Memory Verses

"And I will pray the Father, and He will give you another Helper, that He may abide with you forever—the Spirit of truth..."

—John 14:16–17 (NKJV)

"Not by might nor by power, but by My Spirit,' says the Lord of hosts."

—Zechariah 4:6 (NKJV)

❦ Introduction

You weren't meant to live the Christian life on your own. You weren't meant to figure it out, fight through it, or fake your way through it. That's why Jesus didn't just save you—He promised to **send you help**.

That help is the Holy Spirit.

He is not a distant symbol or a quiet suggestion. He is a **real person**, fully God, fully present, and deeply personal. He walks with you, speaks to you, teaches you, strengthens you, and prays for you when you don't even know what to say.

The Holy Spirit is the difference between **trying** to live like Jesus and actually **being transformed** into His image.

But many believers stop short of walking in the fullness of what's been promised. They're unsure. Or confused. Or maybe afraid to ask too many questions. This part of the journey is meant to change that.

In the chapters ahead, we'll explore:

- Who the Holy Spirit is—and why He's so much more than a concept
- What it means to be **filled with the Spirit**
- How to **hear His voice** and follow His lead
- What it looks like to **walk in spiritual power, not just good intentions**
- The **gifts**, **fruit**, and everyday transformation He produces in your life

This isn't about hype or mystery. This is about learning to walk with the Helper Jesus promised—step by step, moment by moment.

Because the Christian life without the Holy Spirit?
It's not just difficult—it's impossible.

10.

Who Is the Holy Spirit?

✦ He's Not an "It"—He's God

You've just read that the Holy Spirit is not a distant force—but a living, personal Helper sent by Jesus Himself. But who is He, really? What does Scripture reveal about His nature, His voice, and His role in your life?

So let's look deeper—starting with who He is in relationship to the Father and the Son. Understanding the Trinity helps us better understand the Spirit's presence and purpose in our lives.

Some think of the Holy Spirit as a force, a feeling, or just a symbol of God's power. But the Bible is clear: **the Holy Spirit is a person**—and He is fully God.

He's not a "spiritual extra" you receive if you reach some higher level of faith. He's the gift Jesus promised to every believer.

> "And I will ask the Father, and He will give you another Helper, that He may be with you forever—the Spirit of truth."
>
> —John 14:16–17 (NASB)

✦ Understanding the Trinity: The Roles of the Father, Son, and Holy Spirit

The concept of the Trinity—God the Father, God the Son, and God the Holy Spirit—is one of the most awe-inspiring truths in Scripture. It may seem complicated at first, but the more time you spend with the Word and in prayer, the more natural and beautiful it becomes. You don't have to fully grasp the mystery to experience the reality.

God is one—but He exists eternally as three distinct persons. Each has a unique role, and all work together in perfect unity.

Before we dive deeply into who the Holy Spirit is, let's first understand the beautiful and essential roles of the Father and the Son.

✦ God the Father: Creator, Redeemer, and Abba

The Father had you in mind from the very beginning. He is the Creator of all things and the One who formed you with purpose. When sin threatened your future, He put a redemption plan into motion—sending His own Son to pay the price and bridge the gap between you and Himself.

The Father is not distant or angry; He is loving and just. He didn't want to stay separated from you. He wanted you close. That's why He sent Jesus—and it's also why He sent the Holy Spirit to live in you now.

He not only redeems you—He adopts you. He makes you His own child and names you heir to His promises. That means everything that belongs to Him, He now shares with you as His beloved child.

> "For all have sinned and fall short of the glory of God, being justified freely by His grace through the redemption that is in Christ Jesus..."
>
> —Romans 3:23–24 (KJV)

> "You received God's Spirit when He adopted you as His own children. Now we call Him, 'Abba, Father.'"
>
> —Romans 8:15 (NLT)

The Father forgives. He could have chosen to start over with a new creation, but instead, He chose to love and restore you. That's who He is.

✦ God the Son: The Bridge and the Redeemer

Jesus is the visible image of the invisible God. He is the King of Kings, the Lord of Lords, the Name above all names. Everything the Father has, Jesus has. Everything the Father knows, Jesus knows. His purpose is one with the Father—but His role in your life is beautifully specific.

Jesus stepped into the human story to redeem you from the bondage of sin. He paid the price with His own sinless blood so you could be reconciled to God. Sin created a gap no human effort could cross. But Jesus built the bridge back to the Father.

As the Lamb of God, Jesus satisfied the justice of God while demonstrating His extravagant mercy.

> "You were not redeemed with corruptible things... but with the precious blood of Christ, as of a lamb without blemish and without spot."
>
> —1 Peter 1:18–19 (AKJV)

> "Herein is love, not that we loved God, but that He loved us, and sent His Son to be the propitiation for our sins."
>
> —1 John 4:10 (KJV)

Because of Jesus, you are no longer bound by guilt or shame. You are free to walk in grace, truth, and new life.

✦ God the Holy Spirit: The Breath, the Comforter, the Helper

The Holy Spirit is the very Breath of God. He was present at creation, hovering over the waters as the Father spoke life into being (Genesis 1:1–2 NKJV). Later, in verse 26, God said: *"Let **Us** make man in **Our** image…"*—another glimpse of the Trinity working in unity.

The Holy Spirit has always been. He is not new. He is eternal. He came upon Jesus like a dove at His baptism (Luke 3:22). And now He lives in you—guiding, empowering, comforting, and transforming.

You'll learn more about Him in the pages ahead. But for now, know this:

The Father designed your salvation.

The Son secured it.

The Spirit now applies it and helps you walk it out every day.

The Trinity is not a puzzle to be solved—it's a relationship to be lived. And through that relationship, you experience the love of the Father, the grace of the Son, and the power of the Spirit.

✦ The Holy Spirit Lives in Every Believer

The moment you received salvation, the Holy Spirit came to dwell within you. He didn't just visit—you became His home.

He's not reserved for "super Christians." He's the down payment, the guarantee, and the gift given freely to all who believe.

> *"Having believed, you were marked in Him with a seal, the promised Holy Spirit…"*
>
> —Ephesians 1:13–14 (NIV)

✦ Why It Matters

Understanding who the Holy Spirit is will change the way you walk out your faith. He's not just watching over you—He's living in you, guiding, comforting, and empowering you to live a life that honors God from the inside out.

You don't have to figure things out on your own. You're not walking blind.

You have a Helper—and He's everything Jesus promised He would be.

You don't have to know everything yet. Just be willing to know Him. Let the Holy Spirit become more than a name—let Him become your friend.

✦ Baptism in the Holy Spirit: Power and Presence

The baptism in the Holy Spirit is more than a theological concept—it's a gift, a promise, and a powerful experience available to every believer.

John the Baptist said it plainly:

> *"I indeed baptize you with water unto repentance: but He that cometh after me... shall baptize you with the Holy Ghost, and with fire."*
>
> —Matthew 3:11 (KJV)

This isn't the same as water baptism. While water baptism is an outward declaration of your faith and a beautiful act of obedience, the baptism in the Holy Spirit is a supernatural filling—a divine empowerment. It's God pouring Himself into you so you can walk in victory, live in purpose, and reflect His glory.

The moment you received Jesus as Savior, the Holy Spirit came to live inside you. But the baptism in the Holy Spirit is often a deeper infilling—sometimes experienced later. Just as the early disciples had already believed, but still waited in the upper room for the Holy Spirit to come, you too can seek a fresh outpouring, a holy filling that transforms from the inside out.

> *"But you will receive power when the Holy Spirit comes on you; and you will be my witnesses..."*
>
> —Acts 1:8 (NIV)

This baptism brings boldness. It brings clarity. It brings fire—not destructive fire, but refining, purifying, empowering fire. When God filled the believers at Pentecost, they didn't just feel His presence—they were changed by it.

Sometimes people are filled quietly in prayer. Sometimes it happens through the laying on of hands (see Acts 8:17). It might come in a church service, in your car, or in the quiet of your bedroom. God is not limited to a moment or method.

The baptism in the Holy Spirit isn't something you have to work for. It's a gift. All you have to do is ask and receive.

> *"If you then, though you are evil, know how to give good gifts to your children, how much more will your Father in heaven give the Holy Spirit to those who ask Him!"*
>
> —Luke 11:13 (NIV)

📚 For Further Reading

- **John 14:16–17, 26**—The Holy Spirit is our Helper and Teacher
- **Genesis 1:1–2, 26**—The Spirit present at creation
- **Matthew 3:11**—Baptized with the Holy Spirit and fire
- **Acts 1:8**—Power to be witnesses
- **Ephesians 1:13–14**—Sealed with the Holy Spirit
- **1 Corinthians 3:16**—The Spirit dwells in you
- **Romans 8:11**—The Spirit who raised Jesus gives life
- **Luke 11:13**—The Father gives the Holy Spirit to those who ask
- **2 Corinthians 13:14**—Fellowship with the Holy Spirit

Reflection Questions

1. How have you thought about the Holy Spirit in the past? Has your understanding changed after reading this chapter?

2. What does it mean to you that God's Spirit actually lives inside you?

3. How might recognizing the Holy Spirit as a person—not a force—affect your relationship with Him?

11.

Getting to Know the Holy Spirit

✦ He's Closer Than You Think

When we talk about getting to know the Holy Spirit, we're not just learning about a concept—we're stepping into relationship. The Holy Spirit isn't distant or vague. He's personal, powerful, and present. Understanding who He is will transform how you walk with God.

Let's look at what Scripture reveals about the attributes, personality, and divine nature of the Holy Spirit.

✦ Attributes of the Holy Spirit

The Holy Spirit possesses the same divine attributes as the Father and the Son. He is not a lesser being—He is fully God.

- Omnipotent—He is all-powerful.

    "The Holy Spirit will come upon you, and the power of the Most High will overshadow you..."

    —Luke 1:35

- Omnipresent—He is everywhere at all times.

    "Where can I go from your Spirit? Where can I flee from your presence?"

    —Psalm 139:7

- Omniscient—He knows everything—past, present, and future.

    "The Spirit searches all things, yes, the deep things of God."

    —1 Corinthians 2:10

- Eternal—He has no beginning and no end.

    "Christ, who through the eternal Spirit offered Himself…"

    —Hebrews 9:14

These qualities are not merely theological terms. They reveal the Spirit's ability to comfort you in real time, guide you with perfect wisdom, and strengthen you with endless power.

✦ Personality of the Holy Spirit

The Holy Spirit is not an impersonal force—He is a person with a mind, emotions, and a will. These characteristics make relationship with Him possible.

- Intellect—He teaches, reveals truth, and compares spiritual things.

    "These are the things God has revealed to us by His Spirit."

    —1 Corinthians 2:13

- Emotions—He can be grieved.

> *"Do not bring sorrow to God's Holy Spirit by the way you live."*
>
> —Ephesians 4:30

- Will—He makes decisions and acts according to the will of the Father.

> *"He makes intercession for the saints according to the will of God."*
>
> —Romans 8:27

He is wise, loving, and intentional. He chooses to dwell with you. And He desires your fellowship—not out of duty, but delight.

✦ Nature of the Holy Spirit

The Holy Spirit is fully God—equal to the Father and the Son. He is in constant unity with them, yet uniquely present with us here on earth.

Jesus described Him as:

> *"The Spirit of truth... He will guide you into all truth... He will glorify Me."*
>
> —John 16:13–14

Even though the Spirit lives in believers, He still maintains perfect communion with the Father and the Son. He bridges the gap between heaven and earth, delivering truth from the Father and glorifying Christ in all things.

At Jesus' baptism, all three members of the Trinity were revealed:

- The Son was baptized.
- The Father's voice was heard.
- The Spirit descended like a dove (Luke 3:21–22).

The Holy Spirit is gentle, yet powerful. Holy, yet close. He is God's very presence in you.

✦ How Scripture Describes the Spirit

The Bible often uses symbolic language to help us understand the nature and movement of the Holy Spirit:

- Wind—Invisible but powerful (John 3:8)
- Fire—Purifying and empowering (Acts 2:3)
- Water—Refreshing and life-giving (John 7:38)
- Oil—Anointing and consecrating (Acts 10:38)
- Dove—Peaceful, pure, and gentle (Luke 3:22)

These images help us recognize that the Holy Spirit is not limited to one form of expression. He moves mightily like a rushing wind, rests gently like a dove, and fills like living water.

✦ Why It Matters

Understanding who the Holy Spirit is—His attributes, His personality, and His divine nature—isn't just about gaining theological knowledge. It's about recognizing that **God Himself lives in you.**

You are not trying to live a holy life in your own strength.
You are not trying to figure out your calling by trial and error.
You are not alone in your struggle to grow, heal, or obey.

You have a constant Companion who:

- Knows your heart better than you do.
- Speaks truth when lies feel louder.
- Strengthens you when you are weak.

- Intercedes for you when you can't find the words.
- Empowers you to live a life that honors God.

This matters because it shifts everything. When you realize the Holy Spirit is not a distant influence but a present Person—powerful, wise, and full of love—you stop striving and start abiding. You stop asking God to "be near" and start walking in the confidence that **He is already here.**

It matters because the Spirit brings assurance when doubts creep in.
He brings correction when you're drifting.
He brings fire when your passion starts to fade.
He is not a silent partner—He is an active participant in every part of your life.

And more than anything: **He wants you to know Him.**

Not just as a doctrine.
Not just as a force.
But as a friend. A guide. A holy presence living within you.

Getting to know the Holy Spirit won't just change your theology—it will change your relationship with God, your confidence in prayer, your awareness of truth, and your ability to walk in joy, purpose, and peace.

For Further Reading

- **1 Corinthians 2:10–13**—The Spirit reveals the deep things of God
- **John 16:13–14**—The Spirit guides and glorifies Jesus
- **Ephesians 4:30**—Do not grieve the Holy Spirit
- **Psalm 139:7**—The Spirit is ever-present
- **Romans 8:27**—The Spirit intercedes according to God's will
- **Hebrews 9:14**—The Spirit is eternal

📝 Reflection Questions

1. Which attribute or personality trait of the Holy Spirit surprised or comforted you most?

2. How might understanding the Holy Spirit as a person—not just power—change how you interact with Him?

3. In what area of your life do you need to invite His wisdom, comfort, or strength today?

12.

What Does the Holy Spirit Do?

✦ He's Not Just Present—He's Active: The Works of the Holy Spirit

The Holy Spirit isn't just here "hanging out" in the background. His role is active, vital, and deeply personal. The Holy Spirit plays a major role in your life, especially in how salvation is applied, lived out, and sustained. Without the Spirit, you would have no power to overcome sin, no strength to walk in your calling, and no spiritual gifts to help others.

Grace is the unmerited favor of God—a free gift extended to all of us. The Holy Spirit is the breath and power of that grace, flowing through your life. His presence doesn't just help you get by; it empowers you to fulfill the destiny God designed specifically for you.

Here are just a few of the beautiful works of the Holy Spirit:

✦ The Spirit Anoints

In the Bible, to *anoint* meant to rub or pour oil on someone as a symbol of setting them apart for God's use. In the Old Testament, kings, priests, and prophets were anointed for service. Today, the Holy Spirit Himself is your anointing. He covers, protects, sanctifies, and prepares you for service. He's the oil that keeps spiritual parasites—lies, shame, fear—from burrowing into your heart and mind.

> *"Now He who establishes us with you in Christ and has anointed us is God"*
>
> —2 Corinthians 1:21(NKJV)

✦ The Spirit Restrains

Have you ever tried to resist temptation on your own? It's exhausting. The Holy Spirit gives you strength to say "no" to sin and "yes" to God. This power to resist isn't about your willpower—it's about your surrender. As you submit to God, the Holy Spirit empowers you to overcome.

> *"Submit yourselves therefore to God. Resist the devil, and he will flee from you."*
>
> —James 4:7 (KJV)

✦ The Spirit Convicts

Conviction is a gift, not a punishment. The Holy Spirit gently shows you what's out of alignment so you can return to God's love and truth. He doesn't shame you. He awakens you. While condemnation tears down, conviction builds a bridge back to grace.

> *"And when He has come, He will convict the world of sin, and of righteousness, and of judgment."*
>
> —John 16:8 (NKJV)

✦ The Spirit Saves and Regenerates

Salvation is not about you finding Jesus—it's about Him finding you. The Holy Spirit seeks you out, draws you in, and breathes life into your spirit. Through regeneration, He transforms your heart, makes you new, and restores your connection to God.

> *"Not by works of righteousness which we have done, but according to his mercy he saved us, by the washing of regeneration, and renewing of the Holy Ghost."*
>
> —Titus 3:5 (KJV)

✦ The Spirit Empowers

You were created on purpose, for a purpose. And that purpose can only be lived out through the power of the Holy Spirit. He enables you to walk in boldness, share the gospel, live in worship, and be who God created you to be.

> *"But you shall receive power when the Holy Spirit has come upon you; and you shall be witnesses to Me..."*
>
> —Acts 1:8 (NKJV)

✦ The Spirit Comforts

When life overwhelms you, the Spirit is your Comforter. He comes to calm, soothe, and restore. He doesn't just sit silently beside you—He wraps you in peace and reminds you that you're never alone.

> *"I will not leave you comfortless: I will come to you."*
>
> —John 14:18 KJV

✦ The Spirit Guides

You don't have to rely on your own understanding. The Spirit of Truth leads you into wisdom, insight, and discernment. He helps you make decisions, avoid deception, and stay aligned with God's best for your life.

> *"However, when He, the Spirit of truth, has come, He will guide you into all truth…"*
>
> —John 16:13 (NKJV)

✦ The Spirit Intercedes

When you don't know what to pray, the Spirit does. He speaks on your behalf with deep, divine understanding, bringing your needs before the Father with perfect clarity.

> *"The Spirit Himself makes intercession for us with groanings which cannot be uttered."*
>
> —Romans 8:26 (NKJV)

✦ The Spirit Produces Fruit

The Spirit's work in you is visible. Over time, as you walk with Him, you begin to reflect His nature—love, joy, peace, patience, kindness, and more. These fruit are the evidence of His presence.

> *"But the fruit of the Spirit is love, joy, peace, longsuffering, kindness, goodness, faithfulness…"*
>
> —Galatians 5:22–23 (NKJV)

📚 For Further Reading

- **1 Corinthians 2:10–13**—The Spirit reveals the deep things of God
- **John 16:13–14**—The Spirit guides and glorifies Jesus
- **Ephesians 4:30**—Do not grieve the Holy Spirit
- **Psalm 139:7**—The Spirit is ever-present
- **Romans 8:27**—The Spirit intercedes according to God's will
- **Hebrews 9:14**—The Spirit is eternal

⚐ Reflection Questions

1. Which work of the Holy Spirit stood out to you the most? Why?

2. In what area of your life do you most need His comfort, guidance, or empowerment right now?

3. How can you become more aware of and responsive to the Spirit's leading in your daily life?

13.
Filled With the Holy Spirit

✦ What Does It Mean to Be Filled?

To be filled with the Holy Spirit means to live in continual surrender to His presence and power. It is not simply a one-time emotional experience. It is a relationship that deepens over time and empowers you to live in alignment with God's will.

The Holy Spirit is not a force or feeling. He is a person—the third Person of the Trinity—who takes up residence in the life of every believer. But Scripture also tells us to *be filled* with the Spirit (Ephesians 5:18), suggesting an ongoing process of yielding, receiving, and walking in step with Him.

Being filled with the Spirit is the difference between trying harder and living transformed. It's about letting God's power flow through you rather than relying on your own strength.

✦ The Evidence of Being Filled

When you're filled with the Spirit, something changes. It doesn't always look dramatic, but it is always powerful. You may notice:

- A deep sense of peace or clarity
- A hunger for God's Word
- A boldness in prayer or witnessing
- A desire to worship and surrender
- A spiritual language or prayer gift
- A new ability to forgive or love

This filling isn't about spiritual status. It's about availability. God fills the vessel that's yielded to Him.

✦ A Life of Power and Purpose

> *"But you shall receive power when the Holy Spirit has come upon you; and you shall be witnesses to Me..."*
>
> —Acts 1:8 (NKJV)

The word "power" here is *dunamis*—the same root word we get "dynamite" from. It means miraculous strength or ability. The Holy Spirit doesn't just comfort you—He equips you. He enables you to walk in victory over sin, to love others radically, and to fulfill your calling.

Peter, who once denied Jesus, preached boldly after being filled with the Holy Spirit. Paul, once a persecutor, became a fearless witness. And you, too, are invited into a Spirit-empowered life that goes beyond your limitations.

✦ A Spirit Who Moves in Many Ways

Earlier, we saw how the Bible uses powerful symbols to describe the Holy Spirit: wind, fire, water, oil, and a dove. These aren't just poetic—they're personal.

When the Holy Spirit fills you:

↷ He moves like wind—shifting things you can't see.

🔥 He burns like fire—purifying what doesn't belong.

💧 He flows like water—refreshing what's dry.

⬤ He anoints like oil—setting you apart with purpose.

🕊 He descends like a dove—resting with peace and gentleness.

The Spirit knows what your soul needs. And He knows how to bring it—powerfully or quietly, but always in love.

✦ An Overflowing Life

When you are filled with the Holy Spirit:

- **You live in communion**—not isolation.
- **You walk in victory**—not constant defeat.
- **You are guided by wisdom**—not confusion.
- **You operate in love**—not fear.
- **You Bear Fruit That Glorifies God.**

The filling of the Spirit isn't just for ministry—it's for every moment of your life. In your decisions, your relationships, your challenges, and your calling, the Spirit offers direction, comfort, and strength.

📚 For Further Reading

- **Ephesians 5:18–20**—Be continually filled with the Spirit
- **Acts 1:8**—You shall receive power
- **Acts 2:4**—They were filled and began to speak
- **Romans 8:26–27**—The Spirit helps in prayer
- **Galatians 5:22–23**—The Fruit of the Spirit

🖋 Reflection Questions

1. What does being "filled with the Spirit" mean to you personally?

2. Have you ever experienced a time when the Holy Spirit empowered you beyond your natural ability?

3. Are there areas of your life you haven't yet yielded fully to the Spirit? What might change if you did?

14.

Yielding to the Holy Spirit

✦ What Does It Mean to Yield?

Yielding to the Holy Spirit means giving Him full access to lead your life—not just in big decisions, but in the daily, quiet places of your heart. It's surrender. It's trust. It's letting go of control so the Spirit can have His way in you and through you.

To yield doesn't mean to do nothing. It means to be responsive. It means saying, "Not my will, but Yours," and then stepping forward in obedience—even when you don't fully understand.

> *"If we live in the Spirit, let us also walk in the Spirit."*
> —Galatians 5:25 (NKJV)

Walking in the Spirit begins with choosing not to walk in the flesh. And that begins with a yielded heart.

✦ The Battle Between Flesh and Spirit

Every believer experiences this internal struggle: the old nature pulls one way, and the Spirit calls another. The flesh wants comfort, pride, control, or self-protection. The Spirit invites trust, humility, obedience, and love.

You don't overcome the flesh by willpower. You overcome it by yielding.

> *"For the flesh desires what is contrary to the Spirit, and the Spirit what is contrary to the flesh."*
>
> —Galatians 5:17 (NIV)

Yielding is not about perfection. It's about posture. It means daily inviting the Spirit to lead—and then choosing to follow.

✦ Hearing and Responding

The Holy Spirit doesn't shout to compete for your attention. He whispers. He nudges. He speaks gently but clearly. And the more you yield, the more you'll recognize His voice.

Ways the Spirit may lead you:

- A **sense of peace** or unrest
- A **verse coming to mind** at just the right moment
- A **conviction to act** (or wait)
- A **burden to pray**, reach out, or repent
- A quiet **redirection** that brings clarity

When you respond to these promptings, even in small ways, your spiritual sensitivity grows. You begin to walk in step with the Spirit—moment by moment, day by day.

✦ How to Discern the Spirit's Voice

The Holy Spirit always speaks in a way that reflects God's character—peaceful, steady, and aligned with Scripture. But sometimes the easiest way to recognize His leading is by knowing what He doesn't sound like. The Spirit does not speak through fear, panic, anxiety, or confusion. He does not push you toward pride, selfishness, revenge, or impulsive decisions. He never condemns or shames.

His voice brings peace—even when He corrects. His prompting draws you toward humility, obedience, purity, love, and truth. When something aligns with Scripture, produces peace rather than pressure, and nudges you closer to Jesus instead of further away, it reflects the Spirit's nature. When it stirs fear, chaos, ego, or self-protection, it is not Him. Discernment begins by noticing the difference.

The Holy Spirit's voice will never sound like:

- sudden fear or panic
- confusion or chaos
- shame or condemnation
- pressure or impulsiveness
- selfishness, pride, or revenge
- emotional manipulation or anxiety

But the Spirit's voice will always reflect:

- peace (even when He corrects)
- clarity
- alignment with Scripture
- humility and love
- conviction that leads to freedom
- wisdom, patience, and gentleness

✦ Trusting His Way is Better

Yielding doesn't always feel easy. Sometimes the Spirit leads in ways that don't make sense in the moment. But His direction is always for your good and for God's glory.

When you yield:

- You **let go of your limited understanding**
- You **open yourself to divine wisdom**
- You **cooperate with the Spirit's work** in shaping your character
- You **position yourself** to experience deeper peace, purpose, and joy

> *"Trust in the Lord with all your heart, and lean not on your own understanding; in all your ways acknowledge Him, and He shall direct your paths."*
>
> —Proverbs 3:5–6 (NKJV)

✦ Yielding Is a Daily Choice

Yielding is not a one-time decision—it's a lifestyle. Some days it feels easy. Other days it requires courage, humility, or waiting when you'd rather move. But every time you yield, you're saying: "Holy Spirit, I trust You more than I trust myself."

This is how transformation happens—not by striving harder, but by surrendering deeper.

✦ Yielding Unlocks Spiritual Gifts

When you yield to the Holy Spirit, you open yourself to more than just personal transformation—you also make room for the gifts of the Spirit to flow through you.

Spiritual gifts are not earned or achieved. They are given by the Spirit, as He chooses, for the purpose of building up the Body of Christ and reaching the world with the love and truth of God.

> *"Now to each one the manifestation of the Spirit is given for the common good."*
>
> —1 Corinthians 12:7 (NIV)

These gifts may include wisdom, discernment, healing, encouragement, prophecy, teaching, tongues, and many others. Each one is valuable. Each one is designed to bring glory to God and serve others.

Gifts don't function in isolation—they function through surrendered vessels. A yielded heart is fertile ground for the Spirit to move in power, love, and clarity.

This chapter has focused on listening, trusting, and responding to the Holy Spirit. In the chapters ahead, we'll explore the unique ways He equips and empowers believers to carry out their God-given purpose.

For Further Reading

- **Galatians 5:16–25**—Walk by the Spirit, not the flesh
- **Romans 8:5–9**—The mindset of the Spirit
- **Proverbs 3:5–6**—Trust and direction
- **John 16:13**—The Spirit will guide you into all truth
- **Isaiah 30:21**—You will hear a voice saying, "This is the way"

🪴 Reflection Questions

1. In what area of your life is the Holy Spirit asking you to yield more fully?

2. What's one way you've experienced His guidance when you chose to surrender?

3. How can you grow more sensitive to the Spirit's leading in your daily life?

15.

Tools to Live Holy With the Holy Spirit

✦ Living Set Apart

Holiness is not about perfection—it's about being set apart for God's purposes. You were not called to live holy in your own strength. The Holy Spirit is your helper, your guide, and your power source. He enables you to live the kind of life that honors God—not through rules, but through relationship.

To live holy, righteous, sanctified, and blessed, you must develop a growing relationship with the Holy Spirit. He empowers you to fulfill the destiny and purpose of God in your life. That relationship is built and strengthened daily, as you intentionally make space for Him to lead you.

✦ Five Tools That Strengthen Your Walk

Here are five practical, Spirit-led tools that help you walk in holiness:

1. Read and Meditate on the Word of God

God's Word is living and active. It feeds your spirit, renews your mind, and equips you to recognize the voice of the Spirit. Reading the Bible daily is not just a habit—it's a lifeline.

> *"This Book of the Law shall not depart from your mouth, but you shall read [and meditate on] it day and night... for then you will make your way prosperous, and then you will be successful."*
>
> —Joshua 1:8 (AMP)

2. Pray Without Ceasing

Prayer is conversation with God. It's not a ritual—it's relationship. Through prayer, you receive direction, comfort, and power. The Holy Spirit also helps you pray when you don't have the words.

> *"Pray without ceasing."*
>
> —1 Thessalonians 5:17 (KJV)

3. Fast Regularly

Fasting is a spiritual discipline that creates space for deeper intimacy with God. It quiets distractions, humbles the flesh, and sharpens your spiritual ears to hear the Holy Spirit clearly.

> *"But the days will come when the bridegroom will be taken away from them, and then they will fast."*
>
> —Matthew 9:15 (ESV)

Fasting is not about earning favor with God—it's about removing distractions so you can draw near to Him with fresh focus and hunger.

4. Fellowship with Other Believers

Community is essential. You were never meant to walk this journey alone. Fellowship strengthens your faith, encourages your growth, and creates space to learn, share, and serve alongside others.

> *"Not forsaking the assembling of ourselves together, as the manner of some is; but exhorting one another..."*
> —Hebrews 10:25 (KJV)

Spending time with Spirit-filled believers refreshes your soul and keeps you anchored in truth.

5. Maintain Good Works

Good works don't save you—only faith in Christ can do that. But your good works shine as a witness of His love. They are visible expressions of an invisible God.

> *"And let our people also learn to maintain good works, to meet urgent needs, that they may not be unfruitful."*
> —Titus 3:14 (NKJV)

The Holy Spirit will guide you to serve, encourage, and give in ways that reflect God's heart to those around you.

✦ Why These Tools Matter

You can't live holy without the Holy Spirit. But He won't force His way in. As you read, pray, fast, connect with other believers, and serve faithfully, you create space for the Spirit to move freely in your life.

These tools don't make you more loved by God.
They help you love Him more deeply—and live like it.

📖 For Further Reading

- **Joshua 1:8**—Meditate on the Word day and night
- **1 Thessalonians 5:17**—Pray continually
- **Matthew 9:14–15**—Fasting after Jesus' ascension
- **Hebrews 10:25**—Don't forsake fellowship
- **Titus 3:14**—Maintain good works to be fruitful

✍ Reflection Questions

1. Which of these tools do you already practice regularly?

2. Which one is the hardest for you to implement right now—and why?

3. How could applying these tools deepen your relationship with the Holy Spirit?

16.
Stepping Stones

10 Truths to Carry With You

✦ You're Not Walking in Your Own Strength.

Walking with the Holy Spirit is a daily decision to yield, to trust, and to stay open to His presence. These stepping stones are truths to return to—when you're unsure, when you're weary, or when you're simply learning to listen. Let them remind you of who the Spirit is, what He does, and how deeply God desires to live within you.

1. The Holy Spirit is the Breath of God.

From the very beginning, He gave life—and He still does. You were never meant to live without Him.

2. Father, Son, and Holy Spirit are One.

The Spirit is not separate from God. He *is* God—present, powerful, personal.

3. The Holy Spirit is the manifest presence of God on earth.

He reveals what the Father is saying. He glorifies Jesus. He brings heaven close.

4. You are empowered when you are filled with the Spirit.

You're not just saved—you're equipped. The Spirit gives you boldness, clarity, and strength to walk out your calling.

5. The Spirit is all-knowing, all-present, all-powerful, and eternal.

He sees what you can't. He goes where you won't. And He is always with you.

6. The Holy Spirit has thoughts, emotions, and a will.

He is not an energy—He's a person. You can hear Him, know Him, and respond to Him.

7. The Spirit convicts, restrains, teaches, comforts, empowers, intercedes, and leads.

Every part of your growth is touched by His hand.

8. The Holy Spirit transforms you from the inside out.

You don't change yourself. He shapes you, softens you, and strengthens you as you yield.

9. The Fruit of the Spirit is evidence of a Spirit-filled life.

You grow in love, joy, peace, patience, and more—not by trying harder, but by abiding deeper.

10. You have tools to stay in step with the Spirit.

Read the Word. Pray. Fast. Stay in fellowship. Serve with joy. These aren't tasks—they're pathways to deeper connection.

> *"If we live by the Spirit, let us also keep in step with the Spirit."*
>
> —Galatians 5:25 (ESV)

→ What Comes Next

You've learned to walk with the Holy Spirit—to listen for His voice, follow His leading, and trust His power. You've discovered that you're not alone in this journey.

Now it's time for the next step.

Transformation doesn't happen all at once. It's not just a moment—it's a process. And that process reaches into every part of who you are: your mind, your emotions, your habits, your past, your future.

In this section, *Walking in Transformation*, you'll begin to recognize what it truly means to be changed—not just in theory, but in real life.

This is where the old patterns start to break. Where healing becomes visible. Where growth becomes intentional.

God is not finished with you. In fact, He's just getting started.

PART III

I Thought I Was Changed

Walking in Transformation

"Do not be conformed to this world, but be transformed by the renewing of your mind..."

—Romans 12:2 (NKJV)

🎯 Objective

This section will help you understand what it truly means to be transformed by the Spirit of God. You'll explore how real change happens—not just externally, but in your heart, mind, and character. Through practical teaching and spiritual truth, you'll learn how to partner with the Holy Spirit to walk in victory, maturity, and renewed purpose.

📖 Memory Verses

> "I am the vine, you are the branches: He that stays in me, and I in him, the same brings forth much fruit: for without me you can do nothing,"
>
> —John 15:5 AKJV.

> "Therefore if any man be in Christ, he is a new creature: old things are passed away; behold, all things are become new,"
>
> —2 Corinthians 5:17 KJV.

❧ Introduction

Salvation makes you new. But transformation teaches you how to live new.

Walking with Jesus is not about pretending to have it all together. It's about letting Him do a deep work in you—shaping your thoughts, healing your wounds, and aligning your life with His truth.

This kind of change doesn't happen by trying harder. It happens by surrendering deeper. And it's not a one-time moment—it's daily decisions. Every day, you make multiple choices to follow the Spirit instead of the flesh. Every day, you take one more step away from the old you and toward the life God intended.

As you yield to the Holy Spirit, you'll begin to notice something shifting: your desires, your responses, your identity, your direction.

You are not who you were. And you don't have to live like it.

In this part of your journey, you'll discover what it means to be changed from the inside out—and how to keep walking forward, even when growth feels slow or messy.

Transformation is real. And it's already begun.

17.

The Power to Break Free

✦ Salvation Is the Starting Line

When you said yes to Jesus, you were rescued. That moment of salvation didn't just wipe away your sin—it also unlocked the power to walk in freedom. Jesus didn't just forgive you—He set you free.

But here's the part many people don't expect: even after salvation, old habits, mindsets, and wounds can still linger. You may still feel stuck in patterns you thought would disappear. That's because salvation makes you new—but transformation is a process. And sometimes, that process includes deliverance.

✦ What Is Deliverance?

Deliverance means to be set free, to be rescued from anything that holds you back from the life God designed for you. It's not just for "other people" or extreme situations. Every believer needs deliverance in some area of life—whether from fear, pride, addiction, shame, rejection, control, depression, or spiritual strongholds.

Sometimes bondage comes from your own choices. Other times, it's inherited—passed down through generations. You've heard phrases like, "You're just like your father," or "That runs in the family." Generational patterns can keep you bound unless the power of Christ breaks them.

But the good news is: He can. And He will.

> *"It is for freedom that Christ has set us free."*
>
> —Galatians 5:1 (NIV)

✦ Freedom Is Possible

You are not the only one who needs freedom. The enemy would love to convince you that your struggle is unique, shameful, or too deep to fix. But you are not alone—and you are not beyond healing.

Deliverance is part of your inheritance in Christ. The Holy Spirit will reveal what needs to go, and He will walk with you through every step of letting it go. He doesn't expose wounds to shame you—He brings them into the light to heal you.

There is no shame in needing deliverance. But there is great power in seeking it.

✦ This Is What Deliverance Looks Like

Deliverance isn't always dramatic. Sometimes it's quiet and steady. It looks like a realization, a release, a deep breath of peace. Sometimes it looks like tears at the altar. Other times it's a simple but powerful moment of truth:

"I don't have to carry this anymore."
"That wasn't mine to begin with."
"God is not punishing me —He's rescuing me."

The Spirit might lead you to:

- Confess what you've been hiding
- Forgive someone who hurt you
- Renounce a lie you've believed
- Release something passed down to you
- Reject fear, shame, or self-condemnation

Whatever the method, the outcome is the same: freedom.

✦ You Were Meant to Walk in Victory

You don't have to carry bondage disguised as personality.
You don't have to live under labels or limitations.
You were meant for freedom.

The power of salvation includes the power to walk in holiness, healing, and liberty. As your relationship with Christ deepens and your obedience to His Word grows, you'll find it easier to let go of what doesn't belong in your life anymore.

God's will is for you to be free. Ask Him to show you what needs to change—and trust that He'll walk you through it with grace.

📚 For Further Reading

- **Galatians 5:1**—It is for freedom that Christ set us free.
- **2 Corinthians 3:17**—Where the Spirit of the Lord is, there is liberty.
- **Luke 4:18**—He came to set the captives free.
- **John 8:36**—Whom the Son sets free is free indeed.
- **Ephesians 6:12**—Our struggle is not against flesh and blood.
- **Psalm 34:4**—He delivered me from all my fears.

Reflection Questions

1. What are some patterns or strongholds you've seen in your life or family line?

2. How has the Holy Spirit already begun to lead you toward freedom?

3. What's one area you can ask God to reveal more truth, healing, or deliverance in?

18.

You Are a Three-Part Being

✦ Body, Soul, and Spirit

You are not just a body with thoughts and feelings. You are a spiritual being with a soul, living in a physical body.

From the very beginning, God designed you as a three-part creation:

- **Body**—the physical you; your senses and instincts
- **Soul**—your mind, will, and emotions
- **Spirit**—the eternal part of you that connects to God

Before salvation, your life is governed by your body and soul—what you feel, think, and crave. Your spirit exists, but it remains dormant—longing to be reconnected to its Creator.

✦ What Happens at Salvation

The moment you say yes to Christ, your spirit is reborn. You are made new in the most essential part of who you are. But your transformation is just beginning.

You still look the same. You still think the same. You may even still act the same—for now.

But deep inside, something has changed. The Spirit of God now lives in you, and your spirit comes alive. That spiritual awakening is what begins to renew your mind, heal your emotions, and realign your life with God's purposes.

✦ A Shift in Leadership

Before salvation, your body and soul ran the show:

- Your **body** demanded to be fed, entertained, comforted.
- Your **soul** guided your decisions through emotions and logic.

This is human nature at its most selfish—living by what feels good or seems reasonable in the moment.

But as you grow in Christ, your **spirit becomes your leader**. Your body learns to follow. Your mind begins to be renewed. Your emotions start to come into alignment with God's truth.

This is how transformation happens.

✦ Living in Sync

Spiritual maturity doesn't mean becoming less human—it means becoming whole.

As you continue yielding to the Holy Spirit and applying God's Word:

- Your **spirit** grows stronger.
- Your **mind** is renewed.

- Your **body** learns obedience.
- Your **emotions** become stable.
- Your **choices** reflect godly wisdom.

You become a servant of God instead of a slave to your own desires. And in this harmony, you flourish.

> *"The righteous shall flourish like the palm tree: he shall grow like a cedar in Lebanon."*
>
> —Psalm 92:12 (KJV)

📖 For Further Reading

- **1 Thessalonians 5:23**—Spirit, soul, and body sanctified
- **Hebrews 4:12**—The Word divides soul and spirit
- **Romans 12:2**—Be transformed by the renewing of your mind
- **2 Corinthians 5:17**—If anyone is in Christ, he is a new creation
- **Psalm 92:12**—The righteous shall flourish

📝 Reflection Questions

1. Which part of your being—body, soul, or spirit—has been leading your life most often?

2. How have you seen evidence of your spirit growing since salvation?

3. What's one area of your soul (mind, will, or emotions) that still needs healing or renewal?

19.

Your Second Chance

✦ Born Again, Made New

From the moment you were born, your body and soul were shaped by sin. Not because of something you did—but because of what Adam did. His disobedience in the Garden of Eden introduced sin into the human story, and every person since has inherited its effects.

That's why no matter how hard you try, you still fall short. You've said something you regret. You've chosen yourself over someone else. You've done what you knew was wrong.

So now what?

When your spirit is reborn through salvation, you are given a new beginning. It doesn't mean you'll never mess up again. But it *does* mean you're no longer a slave to your old life. You have a second chance. A new nature. A transformed future.

✦ What Is Transformation?

Transformation isn't surface-level. It's not adding a few good habits to your life or trying to "clean up" on the outside. It's a complete conversion—a spiritual metamorphosis.

God doesn't just want to forgive you. He wants to remake you.

Your thoughts begin to change. Your desires shift. Your old, selfish ways no longer feel like home. That's what it means to be transformed.

> *"Do not conform to the pattern of this world, but be transformed by the renewing of your mind."*
>
> —Romans 12:2 (NIV)

✦ Carnality vs. the Spirit-Led Life

To be **carnal** means to live according to the flesh—following the impulses of your body and emotions, even when you know better. Carnality is not the same as being spiritually immature. New believers are like newborns—growing and learning. Carnal believers have heard the truth but choose to ignore it.

Romans 8 explains the contrast clearly:

> *"For to be carnally minded is death, but to be spiritually minded is life and peace."*
>
> —Romans 8:6 (NKJV)

A carnal life cannot please God. It's a life driven by self—one that ultimately leads to emptiness. But to live by the Spirit is to walk in peace, purpose, and truth.

You *can* live differently.
You *can* change.
But you must choose to be led by the Spirit —not the flesh.

✦ The Metamorphosis

The life of a caterpillar is a beautiful metaphor for what God wants to do in you. A caterpillar is earthbound—crawling from leaf to leaf, just trying to survive. Then, in hidden surrender, it enters the cocoon.

Inside, the caterpillar dissolves into something unrecognizable. Everything except the heart melts down. From that place of stillness and loss, something new is formed. And what emerges is a butterfly—free, beautiful, transformed.

That's what God offers you.

You don't have to keep crawling. You don't have to stay stuck in survival mode. Through the Spirit, your life can be made entirely new.

> *"If anyone is in Christ, he is a new creation; old things have passed away; behold, all things have become new."*
>
> —2 Corinthians 5:17 (NKJV)

📚 For Further Reading

- **Romans 8:1–11**—Life in the Spirit vs. the flesh.
- **Romans 12:2**—Be transformed by renewing your mind.
- **Galatians 5:16–18**—Walk by the Spirit, not the flesh..
- **2 Corinthians 5:17**—You are a new creation
- **Ephesians 4:22–24**—Put off the old self, put on the new.

Reflection Questions

1. In what areas of your life do you still feel like the caterpillar—bound, tired, stuck?

2. What does "transformation" mean to you personally right now?

3. How can you invite the Holy Spirit to lead you in one specific area today?

20.

Making Choices to Grow and Mature

✦ Growth Is a Daily Decision

God wants you to grow. But growth doesn't happen by accident. It takes commitment. Maturity in Christ isn't passive—it's the result of daily, intentional choices.

You can't stay the same and expect to be transformed. You can't drift through life and arrive at spiritual maturity.

Growth is an invitation—but it's also a decision. And if growth feels slow, uneven, or interrupted, that does not mean you are failing—it means God is still working patiently, one step at a time.

> *"Do not conform to the pattern of this world, but be transformed by the renewing of your mind."*
>
> —Romans 12:2 (NIV)

✦ The First Enemy: Yourself

Your greatest opposition isn't always the devil—it's often your own flesh.

Old habits. Destructive thoughts. Pride. Shame. Self-pity. Disobedience. These are internal enemies that work quietly but powerfully against your transformation.

Your flesh resists change. It wants what it wants—now. That's why spiritual growth requires daily surrender. Not because God is harsh, but because your flesh is relentless.

What does it look like to fight against yourself? Recognizing these patterns isn't condemnation—it's awareness, and awareness is where freedom begins.

- You choose selfishly instead of obediently
- You rehearse past wounds instead of releasing them
- You make excuses and criticize yourself
- You set no boundaries or violate the ones others set
- You isolate or surround yourself with negativity
- You blame God or others for the results of your own choices

But the more you allow the Spirit to lead, the less power your flesh holds. It's not about perfection—it's about direction.

✦ The Second Enemy: satan

Your second enemy is the enemy of your soul—satan. He hates the children of God. He hates your potential. And he works tirelessly to block your growth.

Satan isn't stronger than God. But he's a master of deception, distraction, and delay. He plants lies in your mind and whispers thoughts that sound like your own.

The Bible calls him the father of lies. He doesn't just tell you untruths—he twists the truth to make it harder to detect. And if he can get you to believe a lie, he can get you to live it.

"The thief comes only to steal and kill and destroy; I have come that they may have life, and have it to the full."

—John 10:10 (NIV)

✦ How the Enemy Works

Satan uses many tactics to derail your growth. He works through media, relationships, distractions—even through thoughts and emotions. Here's a short list of the ways he operates:

Spiritual Tactics	Mental/Emotional Tactics	Relational Tactics
Witchcraft	Depression	Division
Religion without relationship	Anxiety	Strife
Temptation	Confusion	Rejection
Delay and Diversion	Discouragement	Jealousy
Deception	Fear	Intimidation
Pride	Shame	Bitterness
Addictions	Exhaustion	Distrust
Disobedience	Exploitation of Mental Illness	Isolation

This is not to make you afraid—but aware. You are in a battle. But you are not alone. You have been given everything you need to grow, overcome, and thrive.

✦ Choose to Grow

You don't have to stay stuck. You don't have to let the old patterns win. You can choose to grow—and God will meet you in that choice.

You've been given a second chance. Now you're being invited into maturity.

Let the old pass away. Choose transformation. Choose truth. Choose to grow—as the Holy Spirit leads and strengthens you. This invitation is not a demand to hurry—it's a gentle call to take the next honest step, at a pace God already understands.

📚 For Further Reading

- **Romans 12:2**—Be transformed by renewing your mind.
- **John 10:10**—The thief comes to destroy, but Jesus gives life.
- **Ephesians 6:10–18**—The armor of God.
- **Galatians 5:17**—The flesh and Spirit are in conflict.
- **James 4:7**—Resist the devil and he will flee.
- **Proverbs 4:23**—Guard your heart.

Reflection Questions

1. In what ways have you resisted your own growth?

2. Which tactic of the enemy do you recognize most in your life right now?

3. What's one step you can take this week to grow in spiritual maturity?

21.

How to Free the Body and Soul

✦ You were made to be whole.

Your spirit is renewed the moment you receive Jesus—but the journey of bringing your body and soul into alignment with that new life takes time, tenderness, and intentional growth. This is where transformation becomes practical. Your thoughts, emotions, habits, and reactions must all learn how to follow what God has already done in your spirit.

You are not powerless in that process.

This chapter offers practical, Spirit-led tools to help you walk in freedom. You're not trying to *earn* salvation—you're learning to live the new life you've already received. That means resisting what once ruled you and allowing the Spirit of God to bring healing, strength, and victory to every part of your being.

✦ The Battle Within

Even after salvation, two forces will resist your growth:

- your flesh (old habits, desires, emotional patterns), and
- your spiritual enemy (lies, distractions, accusations, intimidation).

You've already seen these enemies earlier—but here's the truth that matters now:

They don't get the final say.

Your spirit—made alive in Christ—is stronger than both when you walk with the Holy Spirit.

✦ How Wholeness Is Formed

Transformation happens when your spirit leads, your soul follows, and your body obeys. As you choose truth, invite healing, and practice obedience, the Holy Spirit begins to restore what was broken and strengthen what was weak.

This is not perfection—it's partnership. Not instant change—but daily renewal.

God wants every part of you whole: your thoughts, emotions, identity, habits, and desires.

The transformation you long for is not just possible—it's promised when your will aligns with God's will. He wants you free.

If parts of you feel slow to follow, resistant, or tired, God is not disappointed—He is patient and present in the process of healing.

🛠 12 Ways to Walk in Wholeness

These practices are not a checklist; they are pathways that strengthen your soul and teach your body to follow your spirit. They take the transformation from "idea" to "experience."

1. Love the Lord

Loving God means building a relationship with Him. As love deepens, obedience follows. When you love Him, you want to follow His commands—not out of fear, but trust.

> *"If you love me, keep my commandments."*
>
> —John 14:15 (AKJV)

2. Desire to Be Free

Freedom begins with desire. God will never force you to walk in liberty—you must want it. If you're used to bondage, freedom can feel unfamiliar or even frightening. But Jesus already made the way. You just have to choose it.

> *"You, my brothers and sisters, were called to be free…"*
>
> —Galatians 5:13 (NIV)

3. Practice Self-Discipline

Fasting, prayer, and spiritual focus help your spirit grow stronger than your flesh. Your body will resist—but over time, it learns to follow rather than lead.

> *"This kind goes not out but by prayer and fasting."*
>
> —Matthew 17:21 (AKJV)

4. Feed Your Spirit

What you consume affects your spiritual health. Just as your body needs nutritious food, your spirit needs truth, worship, and light-filled content. Be selective—what goes in, eventually comes out.

> *"Blessed are they which do hunger and thirst after righteousness: for they shall be filled."*
>
> —Matthew 5:6 (KJV)

5. Read and Meditate on God's Word

The Bible is not just information—it's transformation. Meditating on God's truth brings clarity, strength, and wisdom. Hide His Word in your heart, and it will guide you when life feels chaotic.

> *"This Book of the Law shall not depart from your mouth... then you will make your way prosperous."*
>
> —Joshua 1:8 (NKJV)

6. Make Godly Choices

From media and friendships to finances and thought patterns, your choices either feed the Spirit or the flesh. Living for God means choosing Him again and again—moment by moment.

> *"If any of you lack wisdom, let him ask of God...*
>
> —James 1:5 (KJV)

7. Fellowship with Believers

You weren't meant to walk alone. God places you in a family for strength, encouragement, and accountability. Find people who build your faith, not drain it.

> *"Not forsaking the assembling of ourselves together... but exhorting one another."*
>
> —Hebrews 10:25 (KJV)

8. Apply God's Word

Don't just read the Bible—live it. The power of Scripture is found in doing, not just hearing. As you apply God's truth to your daily life, transformation takes root.

"Be doers of the word, and not hearers only..."

—James 1:22 (KJV)

9. Listen to the Holy Spirit

The Holy Spirit is your teacher, comforter, and guide. He speaks through Scripture, inner prompting, and peace. Tune in, trust Him, and let Him lead.

"Behold, I stand at the door and knock..."

—Revelation 3:20 (KJV)

10. Resist Sin

Temptation doesn't disappear—but your power to say *no* grows. You've been given a way out. You are not powerless. Keep resisting, and the enemy will flee.

"God is faithful... he will also provide a way out."

—1 Corinthians 10:13 (NIV)

11. Develop Spiritual Gifts

God has equipped you with gifts—tools for ministry, service, and building others up. Don't bury them. Discover them. Practice them. Let God use you.

"For to one is given the word of wisdom... to another faith... to another prophecy...

—1 Corinthians 12:8–10 (KJV)

12. Become a Fruit Bearer

The Fruit of the Spirit isn't just a list—it's the visible evidence of God at work in you. As you walk in love, peace, patience, and more, others will see the character of Christ in your life.

> *"The Fruit of the Spirit is love, joy, peace, longsuffering..."*
>
> —Galatians 5:22–23 (KJV)

These practices aren't about perfection—they're about partnership. God isn't asking you to fix yourself—He's inviting you to walk with Him step by step. Each time you choose to listen, obey, and pursue truth, you grow stronger.

Some days you'll stumble. Other days you'll soar. But over time, the Spirit will begin to shape your thoughts, refine your desires, and lead your body and soul into alignment with His will.

This is what freedom looks like—not the absence of struggle, but the presence of power, love, and transformation in the midst of it. Keep going. You're learning how to live whole.

📚 For Further Reading

- **Romans 12:1–2**—Be transformed by renewing your mind.
- **Galatians 5**—Freedom in Christ and the Fruit of the Spirit.
- **Philippians 4:8**—Think on what is true and pure.
- **James 1:21–25**—Be doers of the Word.
- **Hebrews 10:24–25**—Encourage one another in fellowship.

Reflection Questions

1. What's one way your body or soul has been resisting your spirit—and how might that begin to shift?

2. What does freedom look like to you in this season?

3. Which of the 12 practices feels most urgent for you right now?

22.
Results of Transformation

✦ What Happens When You Keep Walking

Spiritual growth is not a passive activity; you must daily choose to seek God for spiritual growth and actively engage in the transformation process. Change is difficult—but it's worth it. When you commit yourself to walk in God's ways no matter what, and keep talking to the Lord about everything, your transformation will continue.

> *"Commit your way to the Lord, trust also in Him, and He shall bring it to pass."*
>
> —Psalm 37:5 (KJV)

> *"Be anxious for nothing, but in everything by prayer and supplication, with thanksgiving, let your requests be made known to God; and the peace of God, which surpasses all understanding, will guard your hearts and minds through Christ Jesus."*
>
> —Philippians 4:6–7 (NKJV)

As you strengthen your relationship with God through prayer and meditating on His Word, changes occur. Circumstances shift. Your mindset begins to align with truth. And soon, the fruit of your transformation becomes visible—not only to you but to those around you.

✦ Old Habits Begin to Lose Power

Your connection to and desire for sinful habits and behaviors weakens as transformation progresses.

> *"But I say, walk and live [habitually] in the [Holy] Spirit... and you will certainly not gratify the cravings and desires of the flesh."*
>
> —Galatians 5:16 (AMP)

Whether it's addiction, anger, fear, or shame—freedom begins when your will aligns with God's. A friend of mine's journey to quit smoking became a turning point when he admitted he still liked the comfort his addiction provided. When he surrendered that desire and met God's will with his own, transformation followed.

You're not powerless. When your desire for freedom meets God's desire to set you free, breakthrough comes. But transformation is not just about what falls away—it's also about what begins to grow within you.

✦ Christlike Character Develops

Transformation doesn't erase your personality—it refines your character. You begin to exhibit the traits of Jesus: love, humility, patience, wisdom, and grace. These changes reflect your new identity in Christ.

Examples of Christlike Character
Faithfulness • Forgiveness • Focus • Humility
Courage • Compassion • Contentment • Confidence
Integrity • Gratitude • Endurance • Purpose

> *"For I have given you an example, that ye should do as I have done to you."*
>
> —John 13:15 (KJV)

> *"For whom he did foreknow, he also did predestinate to be conformed to the image of his Son."*
>
> —Romans 8:29 (KJV)

As your character is shaped by Christ, your understanding of who you are in Him becomes clearer and stronger.

✦ You Discover Your New Identity in Christ

As a new creation, you are no longer defined by your past. You've been adopted into the family of God. But walking in that truth takes time and intentionality.

> *"Therefore if any man be in Christ, he is a new creature: old things are passed away; behold, all things are become new."*
>
> —2 Corinthians 5:17 (KJV)

> *"But we all... are changed into the same image from glory to glory, even as by the Spirit of the Lord."*
>
> —2 Corinthians 3:18 (KJV)

Knowing who you are naturally leads to understanding why you're here.

✦ You Gain Kingdom Purpose

As your spiritual awareness grows, so does your understanding of your calling. You have a role in God's Kingdom—and the more you abide in Him, the more you'll walk confidently in that purpose.

> *"Thou wilt keep him in perfect peace, whose mind is stayed on thee..."*
>
> —Isaiah 26:3 (KJV)

> *"Our purpose is to do what is right, not only in the sight of the Lord, but also in the sight of others."*
>
> —2 Corinthians 8:21 (GNT)

And as you grow in purpose, you also grow in your willingness to surrender every part of your life to God.

✦ You Live as a Living Sacrifice

Your life becomes a response to God's mercy. Rather than being led by selfishness or pride, you choose surrender. You stop living just for yourself and begin offering your life for God's glory.

> *"Offer your bodies as a living sacrifice... Do not conform to the pattern of this world, but be transformed by the renewing of your mind."*
>
> —Romans 12:1–2 (NIV)

✦ You Know Jesus More Deeply

To be like Christ, you must know Him. Through Scripture, prayer, and obedience, you gain a deeper understanding of His nature. As you walk with Him, His story begins to intertwine with your story. He becomes more than someone you read about—you begin to recognize His heart, His ways, and His voice shaping your own life.

> *"That he might be the firstborn among many brethren."*
>
> —Romans 8:29 (KJV)

✦ Transforming Journey

Taken together, these changes form the ongoing journey of transformation.

Transformation doesn't mean perfection—it means progress. It's the lifelong journey of letting God reshape your heart, renew your mind, and realign your purpose. As you walk daily in relationship with Him, the fruit of that journey becomes visible in your character, your choices, and your calling.

Every day you say yes to the Spirit is another step toward the life God designed you to live—a life marked by peace, purpose, and the image of Christ reflected through you. Keep going. The transformation is real, and it's already underway.

📖 For Further Reading

- **Romans 12:1–2**—Living as a living sacrifice.
- **2 Corinthians 5:17**—A new creation in Christ.
- **Galatians 5:16–18**—Walking in the Spirit.
- **John 13:15**—Following Christ's example.
- **Philippians 4:6–7**—Peace that guards your heart.
- **Isaiah 26:3**—Perfect peace in trust.
- **Romans 8:29**—Conformed to the image of Christ.
- **1 Peter 2:9–10**—Your identity as God's chosen.

Reflection Questions

1. What evidence of transformation have you already begun to see in your life?

2. How does understanding your identity in Christ shape the way you view yourself and your future?

3. In what area of your life is God currently inviting you to grow?

23.

The Benefits of Growing in Christ

✦ Practice, practice, practice

Cultivating a strong and growing relationship with Christ requires an active effort on your part. If you want to be a brilliant pianist, you can't just sit around and never touch the piano keys. Maybe you want to be a skilled basketball player. Well, you have to spend time practicing with a basketball. If you want to fulfill a great destiny, do your part. The result of your commitment to growing in God has eternal rewards.

✦ You experience the sovereignty of God

God is the ruler of the universe. He owns everything and has complete control over all creation. That doesn't mean God controls your every move—He has given you free will, and He calls you to choose Him freely.

You have free will and can make your own choices. It isn't God who causes bad things to happen. You are not a victim of a heartless sovereign deity. God wants you to have peace, rest, prosperity, and authority.

Adam and Eve were given dominion and invited to enjoy God's creation. But when Adam disobeyed, that authority was surrendered to Satan.

Through God's covenant and Jesus' sacrifice, that surrendered authority was restored. As a child of God, you now walk in that restoration. You can reclaim what the enemy tried to steal. In the blink of an eye, God could start over with a different universe—but He chose you to rule and reign in yours.

> "Yours, O Lord, is the greatness, the power and the glory, the victory and the majesty; for all that is in heaven and in earth is Yours; Yours is the Kingdom, O Lord, and You are exalted as head over all. Both riches and honor come from You, and You reign over all."
>
> —1 Chronicles 29:11–12 (NKJV)

✦ You learn to distinguish your ways from God's ways

As you grow in Christ, you start to notice when your flesh and selfishness try to lead. God has a different way. You want to act out, but God calls for grace. You want to lie, but the Spirit reminds you to walk in truth. The world tells you to go for what you want—God invites you into something better. His thoughts are not like ours. The more you grow, the easier it becomes to tell the difference between your thoughts and His.

> "For the word of God is quick, and powerful... a discerner of the thoughts and intents of the heart."
>
> —Hebrews 4:12 (KJV)

> "For My thoughts are not your thoughts, nor are your ways My ways," says the Lord.
>
> —Isaiah 55:8–9 (NKJV)

✦ You exercise patience and learn to be still

Spiritual maturity helps you rest in God's timing. It teaches you to keep showing up, keep preparing, and keep trusting—even when the breakthrough hasn't come yet. Being still doesn't mean doing nothing—it means trusting that God is working even when you can't see it.

> *"Be still, and know that I am God."*
>
> —Psalm 46:10 (KJV)

✦ You identify yourself as victorious

You may not always feel victorious. But your feelings don't determine your identity—God's Word does. Each time you overcome, you build spiritual muscle. Growth doesn't mean you never struggle; it means you keep going. And as you persevere, you step deeper into the victory that's already yours in Christ.

> *"Blessed is the man who perseveres under trial, because when he has stood the test, he will receive the crown of life that God has promised to those who love him."*
>
> —James 1:12 (NIV)

✦ You grow in fruitfulness, assurance, and purpose

If a baby never grows, doctors know something is wrong. The same is true spiritually. As you grow, you'll become more effective, more fruitful, and more rooted in your calling. You'll become a source of strength and encouragement to others.

> *"Giving all diligence, add to your faith virtue, to virtue knowledge… For if these things are yours and abound, you will be neither barren nor unfruitful in the knowledge of our Lord Jesus Christ."*
>
> —2 Peter 1:5–8 (NKJV)

Spiritual growth is not a destination—it's a lifelong journey. As you choose to walk with Christ day by day, you'll begin to see the fruit of transformation not only in your heart but in your habits, your mindset, your relationships, and your purpose. These benefits aren't just rewards for good behavior—they are signs of the Holy Spirit actively working in and through you. The more you lean into His presence, the more clearly you'll recognize His hand guiding you. Growth isn't always easy, but it's always worth it. Keep going. God is not finished with you yet.

For Further Reading

- **1 Chronicles 29:11–12**—God's sovereignty and authority
- **Isaiah 55:8–9**—God's thoughts and ways
- **Hebrews 4:12**—Discernment and truth
- **Psalm 46:10**—Stillness and trust
- **James 1:12**—Perseverance and reward
- **2 Peter 1:5–11**—Fruitfulness and eternal growth

📝 Reflection Questions

1. What are some personal signs that you are growing in your relationship with Christ?

2. Which promise or benefit of spiritual growth speaks to you most today?

3. How can you actively pursue more growth this week?

24.
Stepping Stones

10 Truths to Carry With You

✦ You've Been Delivered for a Reason.

God didn't just set you free so you could feel better—He transformed you so you could live differently. These truths are reminders of where you've been, what He's done, and how to keep walking in the freedom He offers. Let them anchor you as you keep growing.

1. Deliverance is the act of being rescued or set free from bondage and sin.

You don't have to stay stuck in old patterns. God rescues—and He restores.

2. Transformation begins by renewing your mind.

Change starts on the inside. New thoughts lead to new choices—and new life.

3. You have two enemies: you and satan.

Your flesh wants comfort. The enemy wants destruction. But God gives you power over both.

4. You must want to be free, or you will remain bound in your sin.

Desire matters. Breakthrough starts when your will agrees with God's.

5. Deliverance frees you to serve God and others fully.

You weren't just set free *from* something—you were set free *for* something.

6. Walking in deliverance and transformation will allow your gifts to grow and your spiritual fruit to mature.

Freedom creates space for growth. You were meant to flourish.

7. Your transformation will strengthen your relationship with God, and your relationship with God will bring more transformation.

It's a holy cycle—growth produces closeness, and closeness produces growth.

8. Transformation will develop Christ-like characteristics.

The more you walk with Him, the more you look like Him.

9. You will learn who you are and what your purpose is in your new identity as a child of God.

You've been adopted, named, and called. Now you're learning how to live like it.

10. Tools for walking out your deliverance are reading the Word, praying, and spending time with other believers.

You're not walking alone—and you have everything you need to keep going.

> *"He who the Son sets free is free indeed."*
>
> —John 8:36 (KJV)

→ What Comes Next

You've learned to walk in transformation. You've been renewed in your mind, strengthened in your spirit, and set free from the strongholds that once held you back. You know who you are—and you're learning how to walk in that truth daily.

But God didn't just save you to survive—He empowered you to serve. You weren't just rescued from darkness—you were filled with light and given supernatural gifts to reflect His love in the world.

In the next section, *I Am Empowered*, you'll explore the gifts of the Holy Spirit and what it means to live empowered by God. These gifts are not earned—they are given. And they're not just for you—they're for others too. You'll learn how to recognize, develop, and walk in the gifts God has placed inside you.

Because you were never meant to walk in your own strength.
You were created to walk in His power.

PART IV

I Am Empowered

Walking in Spiritual Gifts

"You will receive power when the Holy Spirit comes upon you. And you will be my witnesses..."

—Acts 1:8 (NLT)

🎯 Objective

Part Two and Part Three introduced the character and nature of the Holy Spirit and how He works to transform your life. Now, in Part Four, we discover what He does through you. The Holy Spirit not only empowers you to grow—but equips you with supernatural gifts to strengthen the church, edify others, and walk out your calling. These gifts are not random—they are intentional tools placed in your life for a divine purpose. In this section, you'll explore the different gifts of the Spirit, begin to identify your gifts, and understand how God desires to use you for His glory.

––––––––––– ◆ –––––––––––

📖 Memory Verse

"Now concerning spiritual gifts, brothers, I would not have you ignorant...Now there are diversities of gifts, but the same Spirit."

—1 Corinthians 12:1, 4 (AKJV)

❧ Introduction

As a believer, the Holy Spirit has given you supernatural gifts—tools of grace designed to build up the Church, strengthen the Body of Christ, and encourage others in their faith. These gifts are not earned or deserved. They are given freely, according to the will of the Spirit and the calling placed on your life.

The Greek word for *gift* is **charisma**, rooted in *charis*, which means **grace**. Spiritual gifts, then, are divine graces—empowerments given through the Holy Spirit to fulfill your God-given purpose. They are not signs of spiritual status, but evidence of a Spirit-filled life committed to service, growth, and unity in the Body.

In this section, you'll learn what the Bible teaches about spiritual gifts:

- Why they exist
- How they function
- What your personal gifts may be
- And how to walk in them with boldness and humility

You are not powerless. You are not unequipped.

You are supernatural—because the Spirit of God lives in you.

25.

Purpose of Spiritual Gifts

✦ Presents From the Father

Spiritual gifts aren't random talents or signs of spiritual superiority—they are sacred tools given by the Holy Spirit to build the Church, equip believers, and fulfill God's divine purposes. When you understand what the gifts are for, you begin to recognize how God wants to use you.

These gifts empower you to walk in supernatural partnership with Him—allowing you to participate in what God is doing through the Holy Spirit as He ministers to others. As you serve, your own life is transformed as a natural result of working in step with Him. If you're unsure where you fit or what God placed inside you, that's okay. Many believers discover their gifts gradually as they grow in Christ and step out in small acts of obedience.

✦ What Are Spiritual Gifts For?

Spiritual gifts build up the Church. Not the building, but the people—your brothers and sisters in Christ. To "build up" means to strengthen, encourage, and prepare for something greater. That's what the gifts of the Spirit are designed to do.

Spiritual gifts help believers overcome sin, grow spiritually, and become more like Jesus. They equip you for your divine purpose. Throughout your life, God will open opportunities for your gift to serve others right when they need it.

Without the Holy Spirit, you might overlook those opportunities. But with His guidance, you'll not only recognize them—you'll rise to meet them. And if this feels new or overwhelming, that's okay—God develops your gifts over time. That's how you walk in your destiny.

✦ Spiritual Gifts vs. Natural Talents

God gives both **spiritual gifts** and **natural talents**—and while they may seem similar, they serve different purposes.

Talents

- Often inherited or developed naturally.
- Can be possessed by anyone.
- Grow through practice, discipline, and training.
- Bless others on a practical or emotional level.
- Can be empowered or "anointed" by the Holy Spirit for God's purposes.

Spiritual Gifts

- Given supernaturally by the Holy Spirit.
- Only received after salvation.
- Activated by faith.
- Mature through obedience, practice, and staying grounded in Scripture.

- Serve others on a spiritual and eternal level.
- Always point back to Christ, not the individual.

Important Notes

- Faith activates the gift, but daily partnership with God develops it.
- Talents are not "less spiritual." God is the giver of both.
- A talent becomes a powerful tool in God's hands when the Spirit breathes on it.
- The difference isn't about value—it's about purpose.
- Talents equip you for natural impact.
- Gifts equip you for supernatural impact.

Talents and gifts may function differently, but both come from the same God who created you with intention. When you understand how He designed you—and how the Spirit empowers you—you begin to see how every part of who you are can glorify Him.

✦ Scriptural Example

In Exodus 31, God called and equipped craftsmen like Bezalel and Aholiab to build the tabernacle. They likely possessed natural skill, but God did something more—He filled them with His Spirit, giving them supernatural insight, understanding, and ability for the work ahead.

While the New Testament later defines categories such as the Word of Wisdom and Word of Knowledge, what Bezalel and Aholiab received shows the same Spirit empowering people for God's purposes. Their example demonstrates how a natural talent can become Spirit-anointed, enabling someone to accomplish far more than human skill alone could achieve.

Whether it begins as a talent or as a spiritual gift, when the Holy Spirit empowers it, amazing things happen.

"See, I have called by name Bezalel... And I have filled him with the Spirit of God, in wisdom, in understanding, in knowledge, and in all manner of workmanship... And I... have appointed with him Aholiab... and I have put wisdom in the hearts of all the gifted artisans..."

—Exodus 31:1–6 (NKJV)

✦ Why This Is Personal

You don't earn spiritual gifts. You receive them by grace. God, in His infinite wisdom, chose you and entrusted you with supernatural power—because He wants to work through you. He didn't make a mistake when He called you. He didn't overlook someone more qualified or more spiritual. He picked you on purpose.

And maybe that feels overwhelming. Maybe you've wondered, "Who am I for God to use?"

If so, you're not alone. Most believers wrestle with that same quiet insecurity. But the truth is this: God sees more in you than you see in yourself. He placed something inside you that reflects His heart to the world.

You have something this world needs—something only you can offer. When you use your gifts, you help others walk in freedom, strength, and purpose. You become part of the way God comforts, restores, heals, and transforms lives. The Church grows. You grow. And lives are touched in ways that echo into eternity.

Your gift is not just a tool—it's a calling. A reminder that you are needed, equipped, and deeply loved by God.

📚 For Further Reading

- **1 Corinthians 12**—Diversity of gifts, same Spirit
- **Romans 12:4–8**—Use your gift in humility.
- **Ephesians 4:11–13**—Gifts that equip and unify.
- **Exodus 31:1–6**—Anointed craftsmanship for God's house
- **Matthew 25:14–30**—Parable of the talents (faithfulness in what you've been given)

📖 Reflection Questions

1. Have you ever sensed a moment where your gift—or talent—blessed someone else? What did that feel like?

2. What is one natural talent you have that God could use or has used in a supernatural way?

3. How does understanding the purpose of spiritual gifts shape the way you view your everyday life?

26.

Activating Spiritual Gifts

✦ Activating What God Placed in You

Once you receive your spiritual gift or gifts, you must take the next step: activation. A gift left unopened or unused doesn't serve its purpose. God gave you spiritual gifts on purpose and for a purpose. He is ready to activate what He placed in you—but He waits for your "yes."

Activating your gifts requires faith, boldness, and partnership with the Holy Spirit. You must believe that the Holy Spirit truly gave them to you—and begin using them by faith and obedience. A gift left unused will remain dormant—not absent—but as you step out and trust God, the gift comes alive and begins to bless others through you.

✦ What Does It Mean to Activate a Gift?

Activation means **you take action by faith**. You believe that the gift God placed in you is real—and then you use it. Activation is not a one-time event but a lifestyle of saying 'yes' to the Holy Spirit over and over again.

If you believe you have the gift of healing, begin to pray for those who are sick. If you sense the gift of encouragement, begin speaking life to others. The more you use your gift, the more confident you become—and the more room the Holy Spirit has to move through you. Remember, activation is about obedience, not outcomes. God is responsible for the results—you're responsible for the yes.

The enemy will try to stop you before you start.

He'll whisper:

- "You don't have a gift."
- "You're not good enough."
- "You'll mess it up."

Those are lies. The Holy Spirit does not give gifts based on your perfection—He gives them because of *His purpose and grace.*

> *"But earnestly desire the best gifts… Pursue love, and desire spiritual gifts, but especially that you may prophesy."*
>
> —1 Corinthians 12:31; 14:1 (NKJV)

✦ The Laying On of Hands

Spiritual gifts are sometimes activated through a practice called **laying on of hands**. A trusted spiritual leader—such as a pastor, teacher, or elder—may pray for you and physically place their hands on you to activate or stir up the gift that God has placed inside.

This biblical practice is always respectful and done in order. It's not the only way to receive or activate a gift, but it can be a powerful moment of confirmation and commissioning.

> *"Do not neglect the gift that is in you, which was given to you by prophecy with the laying on of the hands of the eldership."*
>
> —1 Timothy 4:14 (NKJV)

✦ How to Stay Activated

Once your gift is activated, it still needs fuel. That fuel comes through God's Word and prayer.

- **Read and meditate on Scripture.** The more you fill your heart with God's truth, the more clearly you'll discern His voice and direction for your gift.
- **Pray and listen.** A daily prayer life keeps your heart soft, your mind focused, and your spirit in tune with the Holy Spirit.
- **Stay in community.** Other believers help sharpen your gifts and keep you encouraged.
- **Seek wise counsel.** A trusted pastor or mature believer can help you grow in your gifts with wisdom and balance.

Without the Word and prayer, spiritual gifts can become self-centered, ineffective, or even misused. But when grounded in Scripture and guided by the Spirit, they become powerful tools for ministry, healing, and transformation.

📚 For Further Reading

- **1 Corinthians 12–14**—Operating in the gifts with love and order.
- **1 Timothy 4:12–16**—Stirring up and developing your gift.
- **Romans 12:3–8**—Exercising your faith and gifts in humility.
- **Acts 8:14–17**—Laying on of hands and the Holy Spirit.
- **2 Timothy 1:6–7**—Fan into flame the gift of God.

📝 Reflection Questions

1. Have you sensed any specific spiritual gift in your life? What steps could you take to activate or grow it?

2. What fear or doubt might be holding you back from using your gift?

3. How can you stay grounded in Scripture and prayer as you walk in your spiritual gifts?

27.

Manifestation or Expression of Spiritual Gifts

✦ How the Spirit Moves Through You

Spiritual gifts are God's supernatural empowerment given freely to believers. They cannot be earned, purchased, or achieved through effort. Instead, they are manifestations of the Holy Spirit working through you for the benefit of others. The gifts listed in 1 Corinthians 12:1–11 are not just for a chosen few—in every generation, the Holy Spirit distributes them among believers as He chooses. These gifts allow the Church to grow, mature, and walk in victory. Learning how to use your gifts may feel messy at first—and that's normal.

✦ Gifts of Revelation

Revelation gifts are divine insights into the mind and will of God.

These gifts unveil truth that cannot be known by natural means. They include:

- Word of Wisdom
- Word of Knowledge
- Discerning of Spirits

✦ Word of Wisdom

Divine Insight for Divine Purpose

The Word of Wisdom is a supernatural gift that allows you to receive insight into God's will or strategy—especially in situations that involve the future or complex circumstances. It's not based on human reasoning, logic, or learning. Instead, this wisdom comes directly from the Holy Spirit to guide you or others toward God's intended outcome.

This gift helps believers make decisions that reflect God's perspective rather than their own limited understanding. It offers clarity in confusing moments and divine strategy for challenges we could never solve on our own. God may use this gift to speak into someone's situation, prevent a misstep, or prepare for what's ahead—even before it happens.

Word of Wisdom also involves a deep understanding of God's holiness and your role within His plan. It is not about being clever. It's about being connected.

✦ Biblical Example: Joseph

A powerful example of the Word of Wisdom is found in the story of Joseph. Pharaoh had a troubling dream that none of his magicians or wise men could interpret. When Joseph was brought from prison to hear the dream, he made it clear that the ability to interpret it did not come from himself—but from God.

Through divine insight, Joseph not only interpreted the dream accurately (foretelling seven years of plenty followed by seven years of famine), but he also provided a Spirit-led strategy to save Egypt and surrounding nations. This supernatural wisdom moved Joseph from a prison cell to a place of authority in the palace (Genesis 41).

> *"The secret of the Lord is with them that fear him; and he will shew them his covenant."*
>
> —Psalm 25:14 (KJV)

✦ Word of Knowledge

Divinely Revealed Facts for God's Purpose

The *Word of Knowledge* is a supernatural download from the Holy Spirit—an insight about something in the past or present that you have no way of knowing on your own. It's not something learned through study, conversation, or observation. It is revealed directly by God for a specific person, purpose, or moment.

This gift is often used to open hearts, unlock truth, confirm God's nearness, or give insight into something that needs healing, repentance, or encouragement. It can help someone make sense of a current struggle or bring hidden pain into the light in a way that leads to breakthrough.

A Word of Knowledge isn't just "having a feeling" or making a good guess. It's saying the right thing, at the right time, to the right person—by the power and direction of the Holy Spirit. It might reveal a hidden wound, a decision someone made long ago, or even a private prayer they never shared with anyone else. And when that happens, they realize: *God sees me.*

✦ Biblical Example: The Woman at the Well

One of the clearest examples of the Word of Knowledge is in John 4. Jesus was sitting at a well in Samaria when a woman came to draw water. She didn't know Him. He didn't ask for her life story. But in the middle of their conversation, Jesus told her details about her past that no stranger could've known: how many husbands she had, and that the man she was currently with wasn't her husband.

This supernatural moment shifted everything. Her heart opened. She recognized Him as a prophet—and soon after, as the Messiah. Then she ran to tell her whole village.

> *"Jesus said to her, "You are right when you say you have no husband. The fact is, you have had five husbands, and the man you now have is not your husband. What you have just said is quite true."*
>
> *"Sir," the woman said, "I can see that you are a prophet.*
>
> *Then, leaving her water jar, the woman went back to the town and said to the people, "Come, see a man who told me everything I ever did. Could this be the Messiah?*
>
> —John 4:17-19, 28–29 (NIV)

The Word of Knowledge turned a routine encounter at a well into a moment of revelation, redemption, and revival. And it all began with one Spirit-led word of truth.

✦ Discerning of Spirits

Recognizing the Source Behind the Scene

The gift of *Discerning of Spirits* allows you to supernaturally perceive what kind of spirit is influencing a moment, person, or situation. This isn't about guessing or being suspicious—it's divine insight into what's operating beneath the surface.

Scripture commands us to *"test the spirits"* because not every spiritual influence is from God. Some are rooted in deception or pride. Others carry God's truth and power. With discernment, you can recognize whether something is being influenced by the Holy Spirit, a demonic force, or the human spirit.

> *"Beloved, do not believe every spirit, but test the spirits, whether they are of God... Every spirit that confesses that Jesus Christ has come in the flesh is of God."*
>
> —1 John 4:1–2 (NKJV)

This gift protects you from spiritual deception and sharpens your ability to walk in truth. It reveals the unseen battle and gives you the wisdom to respond in alignment with God's will.

✦ Types of Spirits

There are three primary types of spirits this gift reveals:

- **Demonic Spirits**—These are fallen angels aligned with Satan. Their goal is to deceive, destroy, and distort God's truth. They can operate through lies, temptation, pride, or even false light. They are crafty, manipulative, and destructive. But the Holy Spirit gives discernment to recognize their influence.

  > *"So the great dragon was cast out, that serpent of old, called the Devil and Satan, who deceives the whole world..."*
  >
  > —Revelation 12:9 (NKJV)

- **Heavenly Spirits**—These are God's angels on assignment to serve His purposes. They are messengers, protectors, and ministers of God's will. Scripture shows angels intervening in dreams, guiding God's people, and carrying out divine missions.

> *"Are they not all ministering spirits sent forth to minister for those who will inherit salvation?"*
>
> —Hebrews 1:14 (NKJV)

> *"Behold, an angel of the Lord appeared to Joseph in a dream..."*
>
> —Matthew 2:13 (NKJV)

- **Human Spirits**—This refers to the part of us that can connect with God—the inner person made in His image. While our bodies and minds can be influenced by many things, our spirit is what God awakens and communicates with through His Holy Spirit. The human spirit carries intention, motive, emotion, and passion. With discernment, you can recognize when someone is being driven by fear, pride, hurt, or genuine surrender to God.

✦ Biblical Example: Jesus and Peter

Jesus showed this gift when Peter—one of His closest disciples—spoke under the influence of the enemy. In Matthew 16:22–23, Peter tried to stop Jesus from fulfilling His mission. Jesus didn't rebuke Peter as a person. He addressed the spirit working behind his words.

Jesus saw both the man and the spirit influencing him—and responded with clarity and authority. That's what the gift of discerning of spirits empowers you to do.

> *"But He turned and said to Peter, 'Get behind Me, Satan! You are an offense to Me, for you are not mindful of the things of God, but the things of men.'"*
>
> —Matthew 16:23 (NKJV)

✦ What We've Seen So Far

The revelatory gifts—**Word of Wisdom**, **Word of Knowledge**, and **Discerning of Spirits**—demonstrate God's supernatural ability to reveal what you could not know or perceive on your own.

These gifts sharpen your spiritual awareness, unlock truth in divine timing, and guard you against deception. They are the Spirit's way of helping you see, know, and understand what heaven sees—so you can walk in alignment with God's will on earth.

These gifts often serve as a foundation for the others, opening the door to action, obedience, and boldness.

→ What Comes Next
The Power Gifts

The next three gifts are known as the **Power Gifts**—**Faith**, **Gifts of Healing**, and **Working of Miracles**. These are gifts that do something. They go beyond insight into action. While the revelatory gifts help you perceive what God is saying, the power gifts release what God is doing.

They reveal His power in a visible, tangible, and sometimes astonishing way—and they remind us that our God is not only wise, but able.

Let's look next at how the Holy Spirit equips believers to move mountains, heal the sick, and release God's supernatural strength into impossible situations.

📚 For Further Reading

- **1 Corinthians 12:1–11**
- **Genesis 41:1–40**—Joseph interprets Pharaoh's dreams
- **John 4:1–30**—Jesus and the Samaritan woman
- **1 John 4:1–4**—Testing the spirits

Reflection Questions

1. Have you ever experienced a moment of supernatural insight or wisdom? What did you do with it?

2. Why do you think discernment is important in today's world?

3. Which of these gifts resonates with you most, and why?

28.

Power Gifts of the Spirit

✦ Supernatural Strength for Impossible Moments

The Power Gifts are supernatural demonstrations of God's strength through the life of a believer. These gifts—*Faith, Healing, and Working of Miracles*—are not sourced from human effort or natural talent. They are three powerful ways the Holy Spirit works through us—miracles that glorify God and make His presence known in the world.

These gifts often operate together. Miracles require faith. Healing may be both a miracle and a revelation of God's compassion. Faith enables both. Together, these three form the arm of God's power at work in the earth—through you.

✦ Gift of Faith

The Gift of Faith is a divine empowerment to believe God for the impossible—without fear, doubt, or hesitation. It is not natural optimism or general belief; it's supernatural confidence that God will do exactly what He promised, even when there is no evidence.

This kind of faith cannot be mustered up. It's not the same as *natural faith* (like trusting gravity or the postal system), or even *saving faith* (believing Jesus for salvation). The Gift of Faith goes beyond—it's God's faith alive in you. It allows you to see past the limitations of your current circumstances and act on the unseen.

> *"Now faith is the substance of things hoped for, the evidence of things not seen."*
>
> —Hebrews 11:1 (KJV)

The Bible is filled with examples: Noah built an ark in the desert with no sign of rain (Genesis 6–9). Abraham believed for a child in old age. Sarah conceived in her 90s. Moses stood before Pharaoh and led a nation out of slavery. None of these people had any reason—by earthly logic—to believe. But they did. And that faith changed everything.

God is still giving this kind of faith today. You may not build a literal ark or lead a nation, but when God places His faith in you, you will know. You'll sense boldness rising up when fear should have taken over. You'll move forward when logic tells you to stop. That's the gift of faith in motion.

✦ Biblical Example: Noah

Noah is a powerful example of the gift of faith in action. God told him to build an ark in preparation for a flood—something that had never happened before. Despite ridicule and decades of waiting, Noah obeyed, trusting God's word without needing proof. His faith not only saved his family but preserved life on earth.

> *"By faith Noah, being divinely warned of things not yet seen, moved with godly fear, prepared an ark for the saving of his household..."*
>
> —Hebrews 11:7 (NKJV)

✦ Gifts of Healing

The **Gifts of Healing** are supernatural impartations of God's power to restore physical, emotional, or mental health. These gifts demonstrate the compassion of Christ and affirm His nature as Healer. The word *gifts* is plural, signifying that healing may come in many forms, through many methods, and for many needs.

To operate in this gift, you must believe that God is still Healer today—and that He delights to bring wholeness in ways that honor His wisdom and timing. The gifts of healing reveal God's heart to make His people whole.

> *"But He was wounded for our transgressions, He was bruised for our iniquities; the chastisement for our peace was upon Him, and by His stripes we are healed."*
>
> —Isaiah 53:5 (NKJV)

Every lash Jesus received before the cross carried purpose. Some have noted that medical experts often group diseases into major categories and have connected this symbolically to the stripes Jesus bore. Whether or not that connection is exact, the truth remains: He took our pain upon Himself, securing healing in every area of human suffering.

Healing may come through a word of prayer, the laying on of hands, anointing with oil, or even the declaration of God's Word. Each healing is different because each person and need is unique. Some healing is instant. Some is progressive. And sometimes, healing comes through medicine or skilled physicians—still under the guidance of the Holy Spirit.

> *"Is anyone among you sick? Let him call for the elders of the church, and let them pray over him, anointing him with oil in the name of the Lord. And the prayer of faith will save the sick, and the Lord will raise him up."*
>
> —James 5:14–15 (NKJV)

In Acts 5, Peter's shadow healed the sick—not because of anything Peter did, but because God's presence was so strong in him that it overflowed into the streets. That same healing Spirit is still at work in His people today.

> *"So that they brought the sick out into the streets and laid them on beds and couches, that at least the shadow of Peter passing by might fall on some of them... and they were all healed."*
>
> —Acts 5:15–16 (NKJV)

Healing is not about a show. It's about God's love on display. And whether He heals through your hands, your prayers, or your presence—He is the One who gets the glory.

✦ Biblical Example: Apostle Peter

One of the most striking examples of the gifts of healing is found in the ministry of the Apostle Peter. In Acts 3, Peter and John encountered a man lame from birth, sitting at the temple gate. Instead of giving him money, Peter declared healing in the name of Jesus—and the man immediately stood, walked, and praised God. This act of healing astonished the crowd and opened the door for Peter to preach the gospel.

> *"Then Peter said, 'Silver and gold have I none; but such as I have give I thee: In the name of Jesus Christ of Nazareth rise up and walk.' And he took him by the right hand, and lifted him up: and immediately his feet and ankle bones received strength."*
>
> —Acts 3:6–7 (KJV)

✦ Working of Miracles

The *working of miracles* is a supernatural act that defies natural law. It is a divine intervention by God that interrupts the ordinary course of nature to bring about His will.

This gift is not limited to healing or provision—it encompasses any instance where God's power transcends what's humanly possible. Miracles can look like physical impossibilities, divine protection, supernatural provision, or dramatic deliverance.

In the Bible, we see this gift at work when **Jesus turned water into wine** (John 2:1–11), **fed the five thousand** with a few loaves and fish (Matthew 14:13–21), or **raised Lazarus from the dead** (John 11:1–44). The gift of miracles was also demonstrated in the Old Testament when **Moses parted the Red Sea** by God's instruction (Exodus 14:21–22), allowing Israel to walk across on dry ground.

> *"Jesus said to them, 'Fill the waterpots with water.' And they filled them up to the brim. And He said to them, 'Draw some out now, and take it to the master of the feast.' ... When the master of the feast had tasted the water that was made wine ... he called the bridegroom."*
>
> —John 2:7–9 (NKJV)

Miracles override time, logic, and scientific explanation. They are not magic tricks or emotional hype—they are God's power on display, revealing His presence and authority. This gift stirs awe, strengthens faith, and draws people to the reality of God.

Just like the gifts of healing and faith, the working of miracles often functions in partnership with the others. A miracle may require a gift of faith to be spoken and believed. And healing may happen as a result of a miraculous intervention. These three power gifts are beautifully interconnected and often flow together to accomplish the will of God.

✦ Biblical Example: Feeding the 5,000+

One well-known example of the working of miracles is when Jesus fed over 5,000 people with just five loaves of bread and two fish. This act was not only supernatural provision—it revealed His identity and increased faith in the hearts of many. It also demonstrated the purpose of miracles: to glorify God and meet the needs of His people in ways human strength could never achieve.

> *"And Jesus took the loaves; and when he had given thanks, he distributed to the disciples, and the disciples to them that were set down; and likewise of the fishes as much as they would."*
>
> —John 6:11 (KJV)

✦ Walking in Power

The gifts of faith, healing, and miracles are supernatural expressions of God's power working in and through His people. These gifts are not reserved for elite Christians—they are available to all believers who are willing to trust God, listen for His voice, and step out in faith. They often work together, flowing in tandem to meet real needs, bring restoration, and reveal the goodness of God.

Your job is not to perform miracles by your own power—it's to partner with the Holy Spirit and say yes when He invites you to move. Whether you speak healing over someone, believe for the impossible, or witness a miraculous breakthrough, these power gifts are meant to glorify Jesus, edify His people, and ignite deeper faith.

→ What Comes Next

In the next chapter, we'll explore the **Gifts of Inspiration**—prophecy, diverse kinds of tongues, and interpretation of tongues. These gifts often speak directly to people's hearts, bringing encouragement, direction, and confirmation. They help build up the church by releasing God's voice with clarity and compassion.

For Further Reading

- **Hebrews 11**—The "Hall of Faith"
- **Genesis 6–9**—The story of Noah's faith
- **Isaiah 53**—Messianic prophecy about Jesus' sacrifice
- **Acts 3:1–10**—Healing at the Beautiful Gate
- **Matthew 14:22–33**—Jesus and Peter walk on water
- **John 11**—Jesus raises Lazarus from the dead

📝 Reflection Questions

1. Which of the three power gifts stirs something in you—and why?

2. Have you ever witnessed or experienced a healing or miracle? How did it affect your faith?

3. What would it look like to begin partnering with the Holy Spirit in one of these gifts?

29.

Gifts of Inspiration

✦ Speaking Life into the Body of Christ

The gifts of inspiration—also called utterance or expression gifts—are given by the Holy Spirit to edify, exhort, and comfort the Church. These are vocal gifts that often manifest in corporate worship settings or gatherings of believers. They are God's way of speaking through His people to encourage hearts, bring clarity, stir up faith, and call His people to action. These gifts are: **Prophecy, Different Kinds of Tongues**, and **Interpretation of Tongues**.

> *"But he who prophesies speaks edification and exhortation and comfort to men. He who speaks in a tongue edifies himself, but he who prophesies edifies the church."*
>
> —1 Corinthians 14:3–4 (NKJV)

✦ Gift of Prophecy

The gift of prophecy is a supernatural message from God delivered through a person by the power of the Holy Spirit. Prophecy is not based on personal opinions or human predictions—it is divine communication from the heart of God to His people. Its purpose is to encourage, uplift, correct, strengthen, and inspire others toward holiness and faith.

Prophecy may expose hidden sin, offer encouragement during a difficult season, reveal spiritual truth, or even unveil a portion of someone's destiny. It may speak of things to come or help the Church respond rightly to what is happening now. But no matter the message, prophecy will always align with Scripture and the character of God.

This gift isn't reserved for pastors or prophets alone. Any Spirit-filled believer can be used in the gift of prophecy. Even children can prophesy when prompted by the Holy Spirit.

Prophetic words may come through speaking, dreams, visions, or even angelic encounters—just as we see throughout the Bible. The key is learning to discern what is from God and what is not. Prophecy should never contradict God's Word and should never be used to manipulate or control. If someone gives you a "prophetic word" that goes against the character of God or the teachings of Scripture, it must be tested and not automatically received as truth.

> *"He that prophesies edifies the church."*
>
> —1 Corinthians 14:4 (KJV)

✦ Biblical Example: Agabus

One of the clearest prophetic examples in the New Testament is the prophet **Agabus**. In Acts 11, Agabus stood among the early believers and prophesied a coming famine that would affect the entire Roman world. His prophecy was accurate and timely, allowing the church to prepare and respond with generosity and care for others. Agabus spoke again in Acts 21, accurately foretelling that Paul would be bound and handed over to the

Gentiles. His words didn't come from guesswork—they were supernatural revelations meant to prepare and strengthen the church.

> *"And one of them named Agabus stood up and showed by the Spirit that there was going to be a great famine throughout all the world, which also happened in the days of Claudius Caesar."*
>
> —Acts 11:28 (NKJV)

✦ Gift of Tongues

The gift of tongues is a supernatural language given by the Holy Spirit. It is not a learned human language, nor is it random babble—it is a divine form of speech that carries spiritual power and meaning.

There are two main types of tongues:

1. **Private Prayer Language**—A personal language between the believer and God, often used in private prayer and worship.
2. **Public Tongue**—A message spoken aloud by a believer in a gathering, which is meant to be followed by an interpretation.

The gift of tongues was first demonstrated publicly on the Day of Pentecost. Believers spoke in languages they had never learned, yet listeners from other nations heard and understood the wonderful works of God in their own tongues.

> *"And these signs shall follow them that believe... they shall speak with new tongues."*
>
> —Mark 16:17 (KJV)

Speaking in tongues is powerful, but Scripture teaches that if a tongue is spoken aloud in a public setting, there must also be interpretation so that the body of Christ is built up and not confused.

> *"For he who speaks in a tongue does not speak to men but to God, for no one understands him... However, in the spirit he speaks mysteries."*
>
> —1 Corinthians 14:2 (NKJV)

✦ Biblical Example: Disciples Filled

The most well-known biblical example of the gift of tongues occurred on the **Day of Pentecost**. After Jesus ascended into heaven, His followers gathered in one place as instructed. Suddenly, the Holy Spirit was poured out, and everyone present began to speak in languages they had never learned. These were real, recognizable languages spoken by people from many nations who had come to Jerusalem. They each heard the disciples "declaring the wonders of God" in their own tongue. It was a supernatural moment that marked the birth of the Church and demonstrated the power and purpose of this gift: to glorify God and draw people to the gospel.

> *"And they were all filled with the Holy Spirit and began to speak with other tongues, as the Spirit gave them utterance. ...And how is it that we hear, each in our own language in which we were born? ...we hear them speaking in our own tongues the wonderful works of God."*
>
> —Acts 2:4, 8, 11 (NKJV)

✦ Interpretation of Tongues

The gift of interpretation of tongues allows someone to understand and communicate the meaning of a message given in an unknown tongue. This is not a word-for-word translation—it's a Spirit-led interpretation that captures the heart of what God is saying.

This gift is crucial when tongues are spoken in public. Without interpretation, the message may confuse rather than edify. But when interpretation flows in harmony with the gift of tongues, it brings clarity, encouragement, and spiritual insight to the whole group.

Just as with prophecy, interpretation must align with God's Word. It is not drawn from the mind or natural knowledge, but from the Spirit. Operating in this gift requires faith, spiritual maturity, and submission to the order of God's presence.

> *"If anyone speaks in a tongue, let there be two or at the most three, each in turn, and let one interpret. But if there is no interpreter, let him keep silent in church, and let him speak to himself and to God."*
>
> —1 Corinthians 14:27–28 (NKJV)

✦ Biblical Example: Apostle Paul

The Apostle Paul instructed the early church to pursue not only the gift of tongues but also its interpretation. He made it clear that interpretation was essential when tongues were spoken in public, so that the message could be understood and received by all. Though anyone can interpret, Paul even encouraged the person speaking in tongues to pray for the ability to interpret, highlighting that this gift is accessible and should be sought after in love and humility.

> *"If any speak in a tongue, let there be only two or at most three, and each in turn, and let someone interpret."*
>
> —1 Corinthians 14:27 (ESV)

> *"Therefore, one who speaks in a tongue should pray that he may interpret."*
>
> —1 Corinthians 14:13 (ESV)

✦ Speaking Life

The gifts of inspiration—prophecy, diverse kinds of tongues, and interpretation of tongues—demonstrate God's deep desire to communicate with His people. These gifts bring encouragement, conviction, and clarity when exercised with humility, love, and spiritual maturity. Though they may seem mysterious, they are deeply personal and powerful, allowing the body of Christ to be strengthened, aligned with God's heart, and prepared for every good work.

→ What Comes Next

The gifts you've just explored are often expressed in **public or group settings**, but God also works powerfully through gifts that shape our **day-to-day attitudes and actions**. These are often referred to as **Motivational Gifts**—the ways God uniquely wires each believer to think, respond, and serve. In the next chapter, we'll uncover these beautifully practical and purpose-driven gifts and how they reflect the heartbeat of God through your personality and perspective.

📚 For Further Reading

- **1 Corinthians 12–14**—Spiritual Gifts
- **Acts 2:1–12** —The Day of Pentecost
- **Romans 12:6–8** —Prophecy as a motivational gift
- **Joel 2:28–29** —Prophecy in the last days
- **1 Thessalonians 5:19–21** —Test the prophecies

📝 Reflection Questions

1. Have you ever received a word of prophecy that confirmed something God had already been speaking to you?

2. How do you feel about the gift of tongues—does it stir curiosity, confusion, or a desire to understand more?

3. Are you open to being used by the Holy Spirit in one of these vocal gifts? Why or why not?

30.
Motivational Gifts

✦ How God Wired You to Serve

God's creativity didn't stop at creation—He designed you with a unique wiring, purpose, and spiritual motivation. These gifts shape how you see the world, how you relate to others, and how you serve the body of Christ. Motivational gifts are internal drivers—often woven into your personality and lived out through how you respond to needs and opportunities around you.

These gifts are listed in Romans 12:6–8, and while they differ from the nine spiritual gifts of 1 Corinthians 12, they are no less supernatural. These are not just talents—they are divinely embedded motivations that help shape your role in the Church.

✦ What Are Motivational Gifts?

The motivational gifts reflect how God designed your inner response to the world and people around you. They affect the *why* behind your service.

You may naturally gravitate toward encouraging others, quietly serving behind the scenes, or generously giving without recognition. These are not random preferences—they are spiritual gifts at work in you.

> *"Having then gifts differing according to the grace that is given to us, let us use them: if prophecy, let us prophesy in proportion to our faith; or ministry, let us use it in our ministering; he who teaches, in teaching; he who exhorts, in exhortation; he who gives, with liberality; he who leads, with diligence; he who shows mercy, with cheerfulness."*
>
> —Romans 12:6–8 (NKJV)

✦ Gift of Helps

This gift shines in behind-the-scenes service. Though often drawn from 1 Corinthians 12:28, many believers experience this as a deep, internal motivation to serve—making it function like a motivational gift in their daily lives. Those with the gift of helps are often the unsung heroes of ministry—setting up chairs, organizing supplies, fixing meals, cleaning bathrooms, or quietly helping meet tangible needs. Helps is one of the most humble, yet vital, gifts in the body of Christ. It reflects the heart of Jesus, who *"did not come to be served, but to serve"* (Mark 10:45 NKJV).

People with this gift bring order, peace, and support wherever they go—and they rarely seek recognition for it.

✦ Biblical Example: Tabitha

Tabitha (also known as Dorcas) in Acts 9:36–42 is a beautiful example of the gift of Helps. She was known for her acts of kindness and charity, especially sewing clothing for widows. Her practical service had such a powerful impact that when she died, the community pleaded for Peter to come—and God raised her from the dead.

✦ Gift of Exhortation

This gift motivates people to move forward with courage and hope. Exhorters are encouragers who lift the discouraged, strengthen the weary, and speak words that inspire faith and action.

It's not flattery or hype—it's Spirit-empowered encouragement that aligns with truth and reminds others who they are in Christ. Exhorters often use scripture to speak life, and their words carry the breath of God.

✦ Biblical Example: Barnabas

Barnabas, whose name means "Son of Encouragement," was known for his gift of exhortation. In Acts 9:26–27, he vouched for Paul when other believers were afraid of him. He also encouraged new believers and traveled with Paul on missionary journeys, strengthening the early church.

✦ Gift of Administration

Also known as the gift of organization or leadership-through-structure, this gift allows someone to develop and execute strategic plans, manage systems, and coordinate people effectively.

Administrators help ministries run smoothly. They think ahead, set priorities, and understand how all the moving parts fit together. With this gift comes a natural attention to detail and a desire to steward people and resources wisely—for God's glory, not their own.

✦ Biblical Example: Joseph

Joseph demonstrated the gift of administration when he managed Egypt's resources during a time of famine (Genesis 41). His God-given ability to interpret Pharaoh's dream and then create a nationwide food storage and distribution plan saved countless lives.

✦ Gift of Giving

People with this gift delight in blessing others. Their generosity flows from a place of love and joy—not obligation. They steward their finances and possessions wisely so they can give freely when the Spirit prompts.

This gift isn't tied to income. Many with modest means possess the gift of giving because they give consistently, sacrificially, and cheerfully. Whether supporting missions, meeting a neighbor's need, or anonymously blessing a family in crisis, they reflect the generous heart of God.

✦ Biblical Example: Macedonia Believers

The believers in Macedonia (2 Corinthians 8:1–5) are a shining example. Though they were poor and going through hardship, they gave with joy and generosity, even beyond their ability. Paul commended them for their overflowing generosity and willingness to give.

✦ Gift of Mercy

Mercy-givers feel deeply. They have a special sensitivity to those who are hurting, overlooked, or vulnerable. This gift enables people to offer emotional and spiritual support in a way that brings comfort and healing.

Mercy does not enable dysfunction—it offers compassion without compromise. Those with this gift often have gentle demeanors, are good listeners, and radiate the tenderness of Christ.

✦ Biblical Example: Good Samaritan

The Good Samaritan in Luke 10:25–37 exemplifies this gift. While others passed by a wounded man, the Samaritan stopped, bandaged his wounds, cared for him, and paid for his ongoing needs. His compassion moved him to action—mercy in motion.

✦ Gift of Leadership

This is the ability to guide, inspire, and coordinate people toward a shared vision—while honoring Christ as the true head of the Church. Spirit-led leaders don't seek power or position. They steward influence wisely, model humility, and point people back to God.

They don't lead to be followed—they lead to serve. The gift of leadership often overlaps with wisdom, discernment, and administration, but its distinguishing mark is vision: seeing where God is leading and helping others get there too.

✦ Biblical Example: Nehemiah

Nehemiah led the effort to rebuild Jerusalem's wall (Nehemiah 1–6). He organized teams, dealt with opposition, cast vision, and inspired the people to complete the wall in just 52 days. His leadership was strategic, prayerful, and God-honoring.

✦ Motivational Prophecy

This expression of the gift of prophecy is not about foretelling the future like the gift of prophecy in Chapter 28 or holding a prophetic office like we will discuss in the next chapter. Rather, it is the God-given motivation to boldly speak truth with conviction. People with this gift feel an inner urgency to confront sin, uphold righteousness, and call others to spiritual growth. Motivational prophecy is grounded in truth-telling and spiritual discernment, not personal opinion. These individuals often speak up when others remain silent, guided by a desire to see people live holy and authentic lives.

This gift differs from the **inspirational gift of prophecy** (which is a momentary utterance from the Holy Spirit during worship) and the **office of Prophet** (a calling with broader authority and responsibility). The motivational gift of prophecy is a personality-shaping drive to pursue and declare God's truth in everyday life.

✦ Biblical Example: Peter's Anointed Message

Peter displayed the motivational gift of prophecy when he boldly confronted the crowd in Acts 2 after the Holy Spirit was poured out. He spoke with clarity and conviction, calling them to repentance and declaring the truth of Jesus' resurrection—leading 3,000 people to salvation. See Acts 2:14–41

✦ Motivational Teaching

The motivational gift of teaching is the deep desire to understand, explain, and communicate God's truth clearly and accurately. This isn't about being a classroom teacher, nor does it necessarily mean holding the office of a teacher. People with this gift are wired to study, research, and share insights in a way that others can grasp and apply. They are passionate about sound doctrine and often have a strong memory for details.

This is distinct from the **ministry gift of Teacher** (a leadership role in the church) and is also different from natural talents in public speaking or education. Motivational teachers are often the ones who fact-check, who ask deeper questions, and who thrive when they see others "get it."

✦ Biblical Example: Apollos

Apollos is a strong example of someone with the motivational gift of teaching. In Acts 18, he is described as "an eloquent man, mighty in the Scriptures," who taught accurately about Jesus. When Priscilla and Aquila helped him better understand the way of God, he became even more effective in explaining truth to others. See Acts 18:24–28

✦ Purpose in Motion

The motivational gifts reveal how God has uniquely wired you to serve. Whether you lead, serve, give, encourage, teach, show mercy, or speak truth—these gifts shape your personality, passions, and purpose. They are part of your spiritual DNA and help you become an effective and joyful member of the Body of Christ. You may see yourself in several of these gifts, and that's okay. As you grow, your understanding of how they operate in your life will deepen—and so will your impact.

→ What Comes Next

Motivational gifts help us understand *how* we naturally serve. But God also appoints *specific roles* within the Church to lead, equip, and strengthen His people. These roles are often referred to as the **fivefold ministry gifts**—apostles, prophets, evangelists, pastors, and teachers. While motivational gifts describe your internal drive, the ministry gifts describe your **calling** to a function or office within the Body of Christ. In the next chapter, we'll explore these vital roles and how they work together to bring the Church into spiritual maturity.

📚 For Further Reading

- Romans 12:1–8—Living sacrifice & serving
- 1 Peter 4:8–11—Serving with God's grace
- Mark 10:42–45—Servant-leadership of Jesus
- Acts 6:1–7—Delegation in ministry

📖 Reflection Questions

1. Which of these motivational gifts do you see in yourself—or have others affirmed in you?

2. How might God be inviting you to use your gifts more intentionally in this season?

3. Are there any fears, lies, or insecurities keeping you from fully walking in your gifts?

31.

Ministry Gifts

✦ Equipping the Body for the Work of Ministry

There is another set of gifts the Bible lists beyond what we've already explored. Often called the fivefold ministry gifts, these are leadership roles designed to build up the Body of Christ. They are given by God to equip believers, advance His Kingdom, and prepare His people for every good work.

> *"And he gave some, apostles; and some, prophets; and some, evangelists; and some, pastors and teachers; for the perfecting of the saints, unto the work of ministry, for the building up of the body of Christ."*
>
> —Ephesians 4:11–12 (KJV)

✦ Apostle

The apostle is one sent with a divine commission from Jesus Christ to govern, establish, and mature the church. Apostles carry a deep burden to build ministries from the ground up, strengthen biblical foundations, and raise up leaders who will equip others. This gift is marked by a pioneering spirit—a calling to plant churches, teach truth, and ensure spiritual maturity in the Body of Christ. Apostles often function across multiple roles, including teacher, prophet, evangelist, or pastor, depending on what the church needs. Their work is foundational and far-reaching.

An apostle isn't simply a leader with influence or authority—they are commissioned by God, not appointed by people. The Apostle Paul is a clear example. Formerly Saul, he encountered Jesus supernaturally and was sent to build the early church. Through his travels, teaching, and letters, Paul laid spiritual groundwork still used today. While some believe apostleship ceased after the first generation of church leaders, the ministry of apostolic calling is still active and needed today. Through apostles, God advances the Gospel, strengthens foundations, and helps the Church grow into maturity.

✦ Biblical Example: Apostle Paul's Mission

The Apostle Paul was not chosen by man but appointed by Jesus Christ to build the early church. He traveled extensively, planted churches, trained leaders, and wrote much of the New Testament.

> *"Paul, an apostle, (not of men, neither by man, but by Jesus Christ, and God the Father, who raised him from the dead)"*
>
> —Galatians 1:1 (KJV)

✦ Prophet

Prophets communicate God's message to His people. While any believer may prophesy under the inspiration of the Holy Spirit, a prophet holds a distinct leadership office—appointed by God to regularly deliver messages of encouragement, warning, correction, or revelation. Prophets don't occasionally offer insights—they live in consistent communication with God and are called to speak on His behalf.

The role of a prophet includes bringing direction, offering insight into Scripture, confronting sin, and calling God's people back to holiness. A true prophet does not water down the truth or adjust the message to be popular. They carry a burden for justice and righteousness, often speaking hard truths that challenge the status quo. Prophets may foretell future events, but their role is not fortune-telling—it is truth-telling. Their words bring clarity, confirm God's timing, and help believers understand and apply His will.

Prophecy will never contradict Scripture. True prophets align fully with the heart and Word of God. Their messages are a wake-up call, often exposing sin or revealing God's purpose in a situation. While prophecy is also a spiritual gift any believer may exercise, the office of prophet carries authority, consistency, and divine appointment.

✦ Biblical Example: Isaiah

Isaiah was a prophet called to rebuke Israel's sin, foretell deliverance, and prophesy the coming of the Messiah. His prophecies span immediate historical concerns and the future hope of salvation.

> *"And we have the word of the prophets made more certain, and you will do well to pay attention to it, as to a light shining in a dark place, until the day dawns and the morning star rises in your hearts."*
>
> —2 Peter 1:19 (NIV)

✦ Evangelist

The evangelist is one who is gifted and anointed by God to proclaim the Gospel of Jesus Christ with boldness, clarity, and compassion. Evangelists are passionate about reaching those who do not yet know Christ. Whether speaking one-on-one or preaching to multitudes, their heart burns to see people saved and reconciled to God. They are often burdened with urgency—feeling the weight of eternity and the beauty of salvation.

Evangelists are not simply persuasive speakers; they are Spirit-empowered messengers. Signs and wonders often follow their ministry, confirming the truth of the Gospel and demonstrating God's power. Whether they are standing in a pulpit, serving on a street corner, or sharing over a coffee table, evangelists are driven by love for the lost and the joy of seeing people encounter Jesus.

Their message is simple but powerful: salvation through Jesus Christ. Evangelists help people understand who Jesus is, what He has done, and how to receive Him by faith. They carry the heart of God for the broken, the far-off, and the overlooked—drawing people toward grace and transformation.

✦ Biblical Example: John the Baptist

John the Baptist boldly preached repentance and prepared the way for Jesus. He called people to turn from sin and recognize the Messiah.

> *"The next day John saw Jesus coming toward him and said, "Look, the Lamb of God, who takes away the sin of the world!""*
>
> —John 1:29 (NIV)

✦ Pastor

The pastor is a shepherd of God's people—called to nurture, guide, protect, and equip the Body of Christ. More than just a title, the heart of a true pastor is marked by deep compassion and sacrificial love. They care for the spiritual, emotional, and practical needs of the people entrusted to them, often walking with individuals through both the pain and the joy of life.

Pastors feed the flock with knowledge and understanding of the Word of God. They labor to ensure that believers grow in spiritual maturity and are equipped for the work of ministry. While evangelists often reach the lost, pastors disciple the found. They teach, correct, encourage, and counsel with gentleness, while also standing firm in truth. A pastor's leadership is deeply relational—it is less about control and more about care.

Pastors serve on the front lines of everyday ministry. They pray, visit, teach, and stand in the gap. They are often the first ones called in a crisis and the last ones thanked when things go well. Yet, their reward is in the transformation they witness—the lives changed, the hearts healed, the saints empowered.

✦ Biblical Example: Jesus the Good Shepherd

Jesus described Himself as the Good Shepherd who lays down His life for His sheep. This example reveals the heart of a true pastor—selfless, watchful, and deeply invested in God's people.

> *"I am the good shepherd. The good shepherd gives His life for the sheep."*
>
> —John 10:11 (NKJV)

✦ Teacher

The teacher is gifted to explain, illuminate, and apply the Word of God with clarity and depth. This ministry gift helps believers grow in wisdom and spiritual maturity by breaking down complex truths into digestible, practical insights. A teacher is not just someone who shares information—

they are a vessel the Holy Spirit uses to shape understanding and cultivate lasting transformation.

Teachers have a passion for truth and a reverence for Scripture. They study diligently, ask thoughtful questions, and guide others toward revelation. Where pastors shepherd the heart, teachers often shape the mind. Their goal isn't to impress but to impart—to plant seeds of truth that produce fruit in the lives of others.

A teacher also provides balance. In a world filled with emotion, distraction, and opinion, the teacher calls people back to biblical foundations. They help believers navigate culture with discernment and apply God's Word to everyday life. Their ministry guards the flock against deception and builds a church rooted in solid doctrine.

✦ Biblical Example: Moses

Moses was called by God to teach the laws and show the Israelites how to live as God's covenant people. His instruction shaped the foundation of Israel's identity and obedience.

> *"Teach them the decrees and laws, and show them the way to live and the duties they are to perform."*
>
> —Exodus 18:20 (NIV)

✦ Carriers of the Mission

The fivefold ministry gifts aren't about status—they're about service. Apostles, prophets, evangelists, pastors, and teachers each carry a unique role in equipping the church, guiding believers, and strengthening the Body of Christ. These gifts are given by God to nurture growth, maturity, and mission.

You don't have to hold one of these offices to recognize their impact or honor their function. As the church grows, the gifts work together like parts of a body—each one doing its part, each one empowered by the same Spirit. As you grow in your understanding of spiritual gifts, you'll also grow in your ability to discern, honor, and collaborate with the ministry gifts God has placed around you.

✦ Where We're Headed Next

Now that you've seen how spiritual gifts work through the Body of Christ, we'll take one more step into personal application. In the next section, we'll explore how to discover your unique spiritual gifts and use them with confidence, humility, and power. Your gift was meant to be used—and you don't have to wait until you feel "ready." God has already equipped you.

📚 For Further Reading

- *Understanding the Fivefold Ministry* by Matthew D. Green
- *The Ministry Gifts of the Spirit* by Kenneth E. Hagin
- **Ephesians 4:7–16** —The purpose and function of fivefold gifts.
- **2 Timothy 4:1–5** —A charge to preach, teach, and lead with endurance.
- **1 Peter 4:10–11**—Using your gifts to serve faithfully.

Reflection Questions

1. Which of the fivefold ministry gifts do you personally resonate with or feel drawn to—and why?

2. Have you experienced the influence of one of these gifts in your life? How did it help shape your faith journey?

3. What qualities do you see in godly leaders that reflect one (or more) of these ministry gifts?

32.

Discovering Spiritual Gifts

✦ Unwrapping What God Has Placed in You

You were created on purpose, for a purpose. And God didn't leave you unequipped. Every believer is given at least one spiritual gift—often more than one—so that we can build up the Body of Christ and glorify God in the process. Some people discover their gifts early in their walk with Christ, while others spend time exploring, asking, and listening. No matter where you are in the journey, this chapter will help you take the next step.

✦ How Do I Discover My Spiritual Gifts?

Here are a few ways to uncover what God has already placed inside you:

Ask God.

It might sound simple, but it's powerful. Ask your Heavenly Father to show you the gifts He's placed in you. He delights in revealing your purpose and helping you walk in it. Ask—and then take time to listen.

Be Aware.

Pay attention to how the gifts operate in others. As you study Scripture, observe believers in action, and serve alongside them, you'll start to notice patterns—both in what inspires you and what comes naturally to you. What moves your heart? What stirs your faith?

Desire Spiritual Gifts.

Scripture encourages us to *"earnestly desire spiritual gifts"* (1 Corinthians 14:1). It's okay to desire a gift that aligns with how you long to serve. God often places desires in your heart that point to your calling. Don't be afraid to ask Him to grow a gift you feel drawn toward.

Actively Try.

You won't discover your spiritual gifts by standing still. Try things out. Volunteer. Join a ministry team. Step into something new. If it doesn't fit, that's okay—God will guide you.

Aptitude and Assessment.

There are many spiritual gifts assessments that can help clarify your unique wiring. Peter Wagner's *Finding Your Spiritual Gifts* is a paper-based option. There are also many online options that offer quick, accessible insight. These tools are not definitive—but they can point you in the right direction.

Confirmation.

God confirms His gifts through both people and circumstances. Spiritual leaders will often recognize your gifts even before you do. As you use your gifts, you'll see the fruit in how others are blessed—and you'll experience a deeper sense of purpose and joy.

✦ What Happens When I Use My Gifts?

When you activate your spiritual gifts, powerful things happen. The impact reaches you, others, and ultimately glorifies God.

1. **You Will Be Satisfied.**
   - You will walk more fully in the destiny God has prepared for your life.
   - You will draw closer to God as you partner with Him.
   - You'll grow in wisdom and clarity for life decisions.
2. **Others Will Be Edified.** The body of Christ needs what you carry. Your gift isn't just for you—it's for others. When you walk in it, the people around you are strengthened, encouraged, and blessed.
3. **God Will Be Glorified.** Your gifts are from God and for God. As you steward them faithfully, others see Christ in you—and He receives the glory.

> *"As each one has received a gift, minister it to one another, as good stewards of the manifold grace of God."*
>
> —1 Peter 4:10 (NKJV)

And remember: If you don't walk in your gift, the body of Christ misses out. Others are waiting for what God has placed in you. When you say yes, you don't just step into purpose—you open the door for others to do the same.

📚 For Further Reading

- *Discover Your Spiritual Gifts* by C. Peter Wagner
- **1 Corinthians 12:4–11**—A list of the gifts given by the Spirit.
- **Romans 12:4–8**—Motivational gifts explained.
- **1 Peter 4:10–11**—Use your gifts as good stewards.
- **Ephesians 4:7–13**—God gave gifts for building up the Body of Christ.

Reflection Questions

1. What stirs your heart or energizes your faith when serving others?

2. Which gifts are you most curious or excited to explore?

3. Have others affirmed a particular gift in your life? What did they see in you?

33.

Using Your Gifts with Confidence

✦ Stepping Out in Faith, Walking in Love

You were never meant to keep your spiritual gifts hidden. God gave them to you for a reason—to build His Kingdom, serve others, and draw hearts to Him. Now that you've discovered your gifts, it's time to use them with faith, love, and confidence.

✦ You're Not Alone

You don't have to wait until you feel "ready." God isn't looking for flawless people—He's looking for willing ones. The truth is, you may never feel fully prepared or qualified, and that's okay. God doesn't wait for you to feel qualified—He walks with you as you grow into what He's called you to. What He begins in you, He equips you to complete.

Your "yes" is more powerful than your fear. When you take that first step of obedience—even if it's shaky—the Holy Spirit will meet you there with power, clarity, and grace. He will give you what you need, when you need it. Your job is simply to move forward in faith; He'll take care of the rest.

As Romans 12 reminds us, our gifts differ according to grace—but we are called to use them.

✦ Use Your Gifts in Love

Spiritual gifts are powerful—but love is the foundation that gives them meaning. Without love, even the most miraculous gift loses its purpose. Scripture tells us that we could speak with the tongues of angels, prophesy with great accuracy, or have faith that moves mountains—but if we don't have love, we gain nothing (see 1 Corinthians 13).

Your spiritual gifts were never meant to elevate you—they were given to reflect Jesus. That means using them with humility, patience, compassion, and a heart that truly seeks the good of others. Love is what transforms your gift from a performance into a ministry.

Whether you're teaching, encouraging, healing, or serving behind the scenes, let everything you do point to Christ and carry the fragrance of His love. When love is your motive, your gift becomes a vessel of grace that draws others closer to the heart of God.

> *"Though I speak with the tongues of men and of angels, but have not love, I have become sounding brass or a clanging cymbal."*
>
> —1 Corinthians 13:1 (NKJV)

Ask yourself:

- Am I using this gift to serve or to be seen?
- Does this gift build others up?
- Does it reflect the love and character of Jesus?

✦ Serve Where You Are

You don't need a stage, title, or spotlight to walk in your calling. God's purpose for your life is not limited to a pulpit—it unfolds in everyday places: your home, your workplace, your church, and your relationships. Your gifts were never meant to sit on a shelf waiting for the "right moment." They were given to be lived out—right where you are.

Maybe that looks like leading a Bible study or mentoring a younger believer. Maybe it's comforting a grieving friend, encouraging a co-worker, or praying quietly for someone behind the scenes. No assignment is too small when it's led by the Spirit. Every moment of obedience—seen or unseen—becomes a thread in God's greater tapestry of redemption.

The Holy Spirit delights in using willing hearts. When you serve faithfully in the simple places, God begins to open doors to greater influence and responsibility. The story of your calling starts with saying "yes" in the here and now.

> *"Whatever you do, work at it with all your heart, as working for the Lord, not for human masters."*
>
> —Colossians 3:23 (NIV)

✦ Stay Teachable

Spiritual growth never ends—and neither does your learning. Discovering your gifts is just the beginning. As you walk with God, He will continue to shape, refine, and deepen your understanding of how to use those gifts with wisdom and maturity.

Staying teachable means being open to correction, hungry for truth, and willing to grow through both success and struggle. Sometimes, God teaches you through Scripture. Other times, He uses mentors, leaders, or even unexpected circumstances to stretch you. A teachable heart stays soft, humble, and ready to learn—even when the lesson is hard.

No matter how long you've been walking with the Lord, there is always more to discover. The most effective servants are the ones who remain students. Keep asking questions. Keep listening for His voice. Keep letting the Holy Spirit lead.

> *"Instruct the wise and they will be wiser still; teach the righteous and they will add to their learning."*
>
> —Proverbs 9:9 (NIV)

✦ Keep Going

You may face fear, resistance, or discouragement. That doesn't mean you're failing—it means you're growing. Spiritual gifts are often forged and strengthened in the fire of perseverance. Every time you choose obedience over fear, you become more rooted in your calling.

The enemy would love for you to give up—to believe that you're not gifted enough, mature enough, or bold enough. But God sees the end from the beginning. He gave you those gifts on purpose, and He's not finished with you. Growth rarely feels glamorous. Sometimes it feels like stretching, silence, or starting over. But don't give up. Keep showing up. Keep trusting the process.

When God places something in you, He will also sustain it. Your faithfulness will bear fruit in due time—even if you can't see it yet.

> *"And let us not grow weary while doing good, for in due season we shall reap if we do not lose heart."*
>
> —Galatians 6:9 (NKJV)

✦ Walking It Out

Walking in your gifts is not about performance—it's about surrender. The Holy Spirit leads, equips, and empowers you every step of the way. You don't have to figure it all out before you begin. As you move forward with faith, God will show you how to use your gifts with wisdom, grace, and power.

- **Pray before you serve. Stay connected to the Source.** Your gifts are spiritual in nature, so staying spiritually connected is essential. Before you lead, teach, encourage, organize, help, or give—take a moment to pray. Ask God for clarity, boldness, and love. Prayer keeps your motives pure, your heart soft, and your focus fixed on Jesus. When you invite the Holy Spirit into your service, you're no longer operating from your own strength—you're moving in divine power.
- **Partner with others. God designed the Body to work together.** Spiritual gifts were never meant to be used in isolation. God designed the Body of Christ to be interdependent, not self-sufficient. Your gift connects with someone else's gift to accomplish more than either of you could alone. Look for ways to collaborate, support, and celebrate others. When gifts work together in unity, the result is exponential impact and a beautiful reflection of God's heart.
- **Persevere when it's hard. Growth happens in obedience.** Even when you're walking in your God-given calling, you'll face resistance. You might feel misunderstood, overlooked, or unsure. Don't let temporary challenges convince you that you've missed it. Growth often happens in hidden, quiet obedience. Keep showing up. Keep trusting God to bear fruit in due time. Perseverance refines your character and strengthens your dependence on the Holy Spirit.
- **Protect your heart with humility and gratitude.** Spiritual gifts can open doors, touch lives, and draw attention. But remember: the gift is not about you. It's about Jesus. Stay humble, recognizing that your

abilities are grace-given—not earned. Gratitude guards your heart from pride, comparison, and burnout. Whether your gift is seen by many or known only by God, it matters deeply and eternally.
- **Point everything back to Jesus. Always.** Every gift you've been given was entrusted to you for one purpose: to glorify Christ. Let everything you do—every word, every act of service, every prayer—reflect His love and truth. When people encounter your gift, may they see more of Him. Let your life and gifts be a living invitation to know Jesus more.

"Having then gifts differing according to the grace that is given to us, let us use them..."

—Romans 12:6a (NKJV)

✦ Gifted for a Purpose

Spiritual gifts are not just about what you can do—they're about who God created you to be. They are expressions of His love and power flowing through you to serve, build, and bless others. As you discover your gifts and walk in them with faith and humility, you'll experience greater joy, deeper purpose, and stronger connection with the body of Christ. You are needed. Your gifts matter. And now is the time to use them.

📚 For Further Reading

- **1 Corinthians 13:1–7**—Love must lead the way.
- **Romans 12:6–8**—Use your gifts according to grace.
- **Galatians 5:22–23**—Fruit of the Spirit guides gift use.
- **2 Timothy 1:6–7**—Stir up the gift in you.

🖋 Reflection Questions

1. What is one gift you're ready to step into more boldly?

2. What holds you back from using your gifts with confidence?

3. How can you use your gifts this week—in small or large ways—to build up others?

34.
Stepping Stones

10 Truths to Carry With You

✦ Stepping Stones—Spiritual Gifts

This section summarizes the most important truths from this section. Let these be reminders, anchors, and stepping stones as you grow in your understanding and use of spiritual gifts.

1. Spiritual gifts are supernatural abilities given through the Holy Spirit.

They are not earned or achieved. They are freely given by God to every believer.

2. Spiritual gifts are given to encourage, strengthen, and increase the church.

They are never for personal fame or control—they are for the good of others and the glory of God.

3. Talents and spiritual gifts are two different things that sometimes work together.

Talents may come through genetics or training. Gifts are supernatural and Spirit-empowered. God often uses both.

4. Spiritual gifts must be activated in order to function.

Spiritual gifts grow strongest as you step out in faith. You get to believe you've received them, be willing to step out, and practice using them.

5. The nine gifts listed in 1 Corinthians 12:1–11 are Word of Wisdom, Word of Knowledge, Discerning of Spirits, Gift of Faith, Gifts of Healing, Working of Miracles, Gift of Prophecy, Gift of Tongues, and Interpretation of Tongues.

6. Motivational gifts include, but are not exclusive to, the gift of helps, exhortation, administration, giving, mercy, and leadership.

These are drawn primarily from Romans 12 and 1 Corinthians 12 and reflect the ways God 'wires' people to serve.

7. The five ministry gifts in Ephesians 4:11–12 are apostle, prophet, evangelist, pastor, and teacher.

These roles help equip and mature the church.

8. A Christian can carry gifts they never use.

You are responsible for discovering, developing, and using your gifts. God has already placed them inside you.

9. Your gifts will glorify God, edify other people, and bring satisfaction to you.

When you walk in your calling, you'll find greater purpose, fruit, and joy.

10. Tools for walking in spiritual gifts include reading the Word, praying, training, and actively trying out your gifts.

The more you lean on the Holy Spirit, the more confident you'll become in using what He has entrusted to you.

> *"As each one has received a gift, minister it to one another, as good stewards of the manifold grace of God."*
>
> —1 Peter 4:10 (NKJV)

→ What Comes Next

You've begun to live the life God created for you—grounded in His love, anchored in salvation, and guided by the presence of the Holy Spirit. You've seen that faith is not a theory or a timeline to master, but a relationship to walk in day by day. So now the question becomes simple and personal: what comes next for you?

The answer is not more information to absorb all at once. It is a life lived with Jesus. Every morning you wake up, you are invited to walk with Him again—to listen, to trust, and to take the next faithful step. You have the Spirit to guide you, the Word to ground you, and the assurance that God is at work in you even when life feels ordinary or heavy.

What comes next is daily faithfulness. It's choosing to belong to God today. It's opening the Word when you need direction. It's praying when you're weary. It's loving when it costs you something. It's learning to carry God's presence into the everyday moments of your life.

What comes next is steady growth—not rushed, not forced, and not driven by fear. God is patient, and He is faithful. He is shaping you as you walk with Him, teaching you to live awake and attentive to His voice.

What comes next is joy and hope. You are not walking this path alone. The Holy Spirit is with you—your Comforter, Counselor, and Friend. Each step of obedience matters. Each moment of trust has purpose. And every day with God is an invitation to live more fully in the life He has given you.

This is not the end of the journey—it is the beginning of a life lived with God. So take the next step with confidence and peace. The One who called you is faithful, and He walks with you every step of the way.

> *"Now may the God of peace Himself sanctify you completely; and may your whole spirit, soul, and body be preserved blameless at the coming of our Lord Jesus Christ. He who calls you is faithful, who also will do it."*
>
> —1 Thessalonians 5:23–24 (NKJV)

You were formed by God before you ever took your first breath—born into a broken world, but never beyond His reach. A Savior paid a price you could not pay, making a way for restored relationship with Him—salvation by grace. Along the way, He has been shaping you and transforming you—through His Word, through prayer, through every step of obedience and every moment of mercy, by His Spirit. And as you walk toward eternity, this truth remains: you never walk alone.

📖 Scripture References

✦ Memory Verses

Scripture quotations are from various translations for clarity and emphasis.

1. *"For whoever calls on the name of the Lord shall be saved."*
   —Romans 10:13 (NKJV)
2. *"And I will ask the Father, and He will give you another Helper, that He may be with you forever."*
   —John 14:16 (NASB)
3. *"Do not be conformed to this world, but be transformed by the renewing of your mind..."*
   —Romans 12:2 (NKJV)
4. *"You will receive power when the Holy Spirit comes upon you. And you will be my witnesses..."*
   —Acts 1:8 (NLT)
5. *"...for the fruit of light is found in all that is good and right and true..."*
   —Ephesians 5:9 (ESV)
6. *"Therefore, take up the full armor of God, that you may be able to resist in the evil day, and having done everything, to stand firm."*
   —Ephesians 6:13 (NASB)
7. *"This Book of the Law shall not depart from your mouth, but you shall meditate in it day and night, that you may observe to do according to all that is written in it. For then you will make your way prosperous, and then you will have good success,"*
   —Joshua 1:8 (NKJV)
8. *"Do not be anxious about anything, but in everything, by prayer and petition, with thanksgiving, present your requests to God."*
   —Philippians 4:6 (NKJV)

9. *"Run in such a way as to get the prize… They do it to get a crown that will not last, but we do it to get a crown that will last forever"*
—1 Corinthians 9:24-25 (NIV)

📖 Resources for Your Journey

Here are some books, apps, and websites that can help you keep growing in your walk with Christ. These tools are not required but can serve as encouragement, guidance, and study aids along the way.

📚 Books

- *The Pursuit of God* —A.W. Tozer
- *Mere Christianity* —C.S. Lewis
- *The Purpose Driven Life* —Rick Warren
- *Celebration of Discipline* —Richard Foster
- *Knowing God* —J.I. Packer
- *The Case for Christ* —Lee Strobel
- *Experiencing God*—Henry Blackaby
- *Battlefield of the Mind*—Joyce Meyer

📱 Apps

- **YouVersion Bible App**—Multiple translations, devotionals, and audio Bible.
- **Blue Letter Bible**—In-depth study tools, concordances, and original language helps. *(also available as a website)*
- **Bible Gateway**—Online Bible with search tools and study resources. *(also available as a website)*

- **Logos Bible Software**—A powerful tool for deeper Bible study *(best suited for advanced study)*.
- **Dwell**—An audio Bible app that helps you meditate on Scripture.

🌐 Websites

- Bible Project—Animated videos and resources explaining biblical themes.
- GotQuestions—Clear answers to common Bible questions.
- Desiring God—Articles and sermons centered on enjoying God.
- OpenBible.info—Topical Bible verse lookup.

✍ Bible Study Helps

- A **Concordance** (Strong's is the most well-known)—helps find words across the Bible.
- A **Study Bible** (such as the ESV Study Bible or NIV Study Bible)—includes notes, maps, and commentary.
- **Commentaries** (like Matthew Henry's)—provide background and explanation of Scripture passages.

☞ Remember: these tools are helpful, but the most important thing is simply **spending time with God in His Word and prayer.**

Glossary

Simple Glossary of a Few Words from the Christian Faith

Adultery—The act of being sexually unfaithful to one's spouse

Agape—Affection, goodwill, love, brotherly love, a love feast

Angel—Messenger of God

Anoint / Anointing—To be set apart and empowered by God's Spirit for a special purpose; often symbolized by oil in Scripture.

Apostasy—Turning away from the religion, faith, or principles that one used to believe

Apostle—One sent forth, one chosen and sent with a special commission as a fully authorized representative of the sender.

Atonement—To cover, blot out, forgive; restore harmony between two individuals.

Attribute—An inherent characteristic

Backslide—To go back to ungodly ways of believing or acting.

Baptism—An outward sign of an inward change; immersion in water (or sprinkling) symbolizing cleansing from sin and identification with Christ's death, burial, and resurrection.

Blasphemy—Words or actions showing a lack of respect for God or anything sacred.

Bless—To make or call holy, to ask God's favor, to praise; to make happy.

Blessing—A prayer asking God's favor for something, something that brings joy or comfort.

Body of Christ—A biblical term for the Church, meaning all believers together are one spiritual family with Christ as the head.

Born-again—To be begotten or birthed from God, the beginning, to start anew

Carnal—Living primarily according to fleshly desires rather than the Spirit of Christ

Cherubim—Guardian angels, angels that guard or protect places

Commitment—A promise, a pledge

Conditional—Placing restrictions, conditions, or provisions to receive

Conversion/Conversion—Turn, return, turn back; change

Covenant—A pledge, alliance, agreement

Cult—A group whose teachings deviate from core biblical truth, particularly concerning the nature of Christ.

Deliverance—A freeing or being freed, rescue; the act of change or transformation.

Demon—Evil spirit

Devil—Principal title for satan, the archenemy of God and man

Disciple—A follower, learner, or student of Jesus who seeks to live by His teachings.

Dispensation—A period of time, sometimes called ages

Dominion—To rule over, have power over, overcome, exercise lordship over

Elder—A leader in the church who provides spiritual care, teaching, and oversight.

Eros—Erotic, physical love

Eternal—Existing always, forever, without time

Evangelist—Proclaims the gospel of Jesus Christ

Faith—Believing, trusting, depending, and relying on God

Fellowship—Sharing, communion, partnership, intimacy

Forgiveness—To pardon, release from bondage

Fornication—To act like a harlot, to be unfaithful to God, illicit sexual intercourse

Glorification—Salvation of the body, transforming mortal bodies to eternal bodies

Gospel—The "good news" of Jesus Christ—His life, death, resurrection, and the salvation He brings.

Grace—Unmerited favor of God, help given in the time of need from a loving God

Heaven—The eternal home of God and His people; a place of joy, peace, and God's presence.

Hell—Eternal separation from God; a place of punishment for Satan, demons, and all who reject Christ.

Holy—Set apart, sacred

Intercession—To meet or encounter, to strike upon, to pray for another

Justification—Salvation of the spirit, just as if I never sinned

Kingdom of God—God's reign and rule, both now in the hearts of believers and ultimately in the new heaven and new earth.

Messiah / Christ—"The Anointed One"; the promised Savior and Deliverer, fulfilled in Jesus.

Ministry—Service done for God and others, using your gifts, time, and life to glorify Him.

New Testament—Text of the new covenant

Offering—Everything you give beyond your tithe

Old Testament—Text of the old covenant

Omnipotent—All-encompassing power of God

Omnipresent—Unlimited nature of God, ability to be everywhere at all times

Omniscient—God's power to know all things

Pastor—Shepherds of the body of believers

Pentecost—The day the Holy Spirit was poured out on believers (Acts 2), marking the birth of the Church.

Philia—Conditional love, based on feelings, friendships

Praise—Thanksgiving, to say good things about, words that show approval.

Prayer—Communication with God

Prophet—One who is a spokesperson for God, one who has seen the message of God and declares that message

Propitiation—To satisfy the anger of God, to gain favor; appease

Rapture—To be carried away, or the catching away of

Reconciliation—Restore harmony or fellowship between individuals, to make friendly again

Redemption—To buy back, to purchase, recover, to Rescue from sin

Regeneration—To give new life or force to, renew, to be restored, to make better, improve or reform, to grow back anew

Repent/Repentance—Turning away from sin and turning back to God with a changed heart and mind.

Resurrection—A return to life subsequent to death

Revelation—The act of revealing or making known

Righteousness—Right standing with God, integrity, virtue, purity of life, correctness of thinking

Sacrifice—The act of offering something, giving one thing for the sake of another; a loss of profit

Salvation—Deliverance from any kind of evil whether material or spiritual, being saved from danger or evil; to rescue.

Sanctification—Salvation of the soul. Separation from the seduction of sin

Satan—The chief of fallen spirits, opponent; adversary

Sealing—Something that guarantees, a sign or token, to make with a seal to make it official or genuine

Shekinah Glory—A term used to describe the manifest presence of God dwelling with His people.

Sin—All unrighteousness, missing the mark, wrong or fault; violation of the law

Spirit—A being that is not of this world, has no flesh or bones

Steward—A guardian or overseer of someone else's property, manager

Supernatural—Departing from what is usual, normal, or natural to give the appearance of transcending the laws of nature

Talent—A natural skill that is unusual.

Testimony—The story of what God has done in your life; a witness of His saving and transforming power.

Tithe—Ten percent of all your increase

Tribulation—Distress, trouble, a pressing together, pressure, affliction

Trinity—Three in one: Father, Son, Holy Spirit

Unconditional—No restrictions, conditions, boundaries, demands, or specific provisions

Will—Choice, inclination, desire, pleasure, command, what one wishes or determines shall be done

Worship—Giving honor, reverence, and adoration to God through words, actions, and lifestyle.

About the Author

Pamela D. White is a writer, teacher, and encourager with a heart for helping people find freedom and wholeness in Christ. Drawing from her own journey of walking with Jesus through both hardship and healing, she writes with honesty, compassion, and a deep love for God's Word.

Her books are designed to be more than words on a page—they are invitations into transformation. Whether guiding readers through prayer, exploring Scripture, or sharing her story, Pamela's desire remains the same: that each person would discover their true identity in Christ and learn to walk in the power and presence of the Holy Spirit.

When she isn't writing, Pamela finds joy in walking with her dogs and communing with Jesus in the quiet of nature, leading small groups, creating discipleship resources, and encouraging others to step into the calling God has placed on their lives. She believes healing and hope are possible for everyone—and that God walks with us through every step of that transformational journey, never leaving us alone.

You can connect with Pamela online at BloomingDesert.org for resources, updates, and encouragement for your own journey.

www.ingramcontent.com/pod-product-compliance
Lightning Source LLC
Chambersburg PA
CBHW042124100526
44587CB00026B/4171